T0272184

CAMPER FOOD & STORIES

ITALY

CAMPER FOOD
& STORIES
ITALY

LUSTER

ELS SIREJACOB & BRAM DEBAENST

PREFACE: WE'RE *SORRY!*

Yes, that's right. This book starts with a sincere apology to anyone with Italian roots. Because writing a book about Italy, and Italian cuisine in particular, is something that should only be undertaken by an Italian. And yet, we non-Italians had the temerity to do this. Why? Because of love! While travelling through Italy, we fell in love. With the country, its heritage, its culture, its landscapes, the colours, the climate, the Italians … and the FOOD!

The best place on earth

Obviously, we've had these strong feelings for quite some time, since our very first trip to Italy in fact – aeons ago. Since then, we've returned many times and each time we are overjoyed to discover that in Italy you can eat really well anywhere, any time. And don't get us started on their amazing wines. You will almost never be served bad food in a restaurant in Italy, which explains why we chose to hardly share any restaurant tips in this book. Don't overthink it. Let the delicious scents that waft towards you, your curiosity, and chance be your guides. Don't be fooled by the interior: sometimes the best meals can be found in the most rundown places.

Our passion for Italy and its cuisine has only become stronger, our infatuation more intense, after our camper road trips in the summer of 2022. Part of this book is a personal record of these trips. Two different trips, of two families, both travelling in a camper van. Each with their own story, and their own choices. That is why our homage to Italy is selective and anything but comprehensive. Bram and his family explored the west coast, camping along the Ligurian coast and in Sorrento. Els and her husband and their dog concentrated on the east of Italy, spending lots of time in the mountains. There are many regions and places that we didn't cover, and which are not included in this book as a result. Sorry about that! We are already dreaming of a third book, because there are so many Italian cities and regions to which we want to introduce you, where we want to immerse ourselves in the culinary traditions and local specialities. Sicily and Rome are at the top of our list!

Camper food *all'Italiana*

This book is really about all these culinary traditions. The dishes that we prepared in our camper kitchens make up the second part of our book, and the essence of this project. In fact, it has become more of a cookbook than we had originally planned; Italy simply is a never-ending source of inspiration for a recipe writer/food stylist and a food photographer. Superb food awaits in every region. To Italians, their food culture is like a religion. And rightly so! A pasta dish to whet your appetite, followed by a delicious cut of meat with some vegetables:

any lunch or dinner becomes a celebration of good food, thanks to the sublime produce to which Italians have access and the dedication with which they cook.

In every region, we went in search of the most delicious local dishes that you can prepare in or near your camper van. We adapted some of the recipes – hence our opening apology. For example, the pasta dishes on the next pages are listed as main courses, the way we are used to eating pasta in Belgium and the Netherlands. Not because we like it better that way but because we think this is more manageable when you're camping: prepping a starter and a main course seems too much of a faff. But of course, it's your choice. Do what you want. Halve the quantities of the pasta dishes, if you want to serve them as a primo and you have the time to prepare a two-course meal.

Other recipes were included as is, in all their glory, without any changes, just like Italian nonnas would cook them. Some classics are best left untouched. Every recipe that we included in this book, whether we gave it our own twist or not, is all about respect, however. We have compiled each recipe with a lot of love, which is why we are so proud of the result. That is why we hope that our readers, whether Italian or not, will nod approvingly as they leaf through the book and read it. Even more so when they prepare one of the droolworthy dishes on the next pages…

We hope you enjoy reading, looking, and cooking from this book. Or better yet: have a good trip and enjoy the food!

Bram and Els

PS: a valuable tip

We owe some of our best camping experiences in Italy to the **Agricamper Italia** app: a digital guide that you buy and which gives you access to an unlimited number of free stops at sites across the Agricamper Italia network, over a 12-month period. You can stay for 24 hours. The network includes more than 270 farms, vineyards, and idyllic sites across Italy, which make available pitches to self-catering camper vans, motorhomes, or caravans. All you have to do as a guest is introduce yourself, leave everything behind spick and span, and say goodbye when you leave. And if you can, it's always a good idea to buy something in the farm shop – we always do! According to the app's rules, you may not share any names or places. That is why we share our experiences in this book, without listing the addresses.

VIA GRA
NATURALE
€ 5,00

EL*S'S* JOURNEY

The summer of 2022 in Italy was 'our summer' – meaning my husband Mike and me, and our sweet and super-spoiled four-legged friend, Willy. We really needed some time to ourselves and for each other, some peace and quiet, and positive vibes. While we had some mixed feelings about it – going off for a month without our children was quite something –, we fortunately also had access to FaceTime when we missed them too much.

We had previously been on holiday in Italy, travelling to Sicily, Sardinia, Rome, Piemonte and South Tyrol. Returning to the land where *la dolce vita* is a way of life was easy: the language is beautiful, the coffee is ridiculously good, there are ice creams, incredible pastas, olive trees and lemons to enjoy ... What's not to like? We focused on the regions in the east because that part of the country was still relatively unknown to us, starting in the Dolomites, winding our way through the Veneto and Lombardy to Emilia-Romagna and on to Le Marche, Umbria and gorgeous Abruzzo, with Puglia as our final destination. In this book we also share our experiences during an earlier trip to Piemonte, with the whole family in 2020.

Although we mapped out a route in advance and put loads of pins on Google Maps, once there we preferred to follow our gut feeling – and in a country with a phenomenal food culture like Italy, we mean this very literally. Sticking to all those pins only gives you cause for stress, which is exactly what you don't want, when travelling in a camper van and experiencing the freedom that comes with it. All you want is to have no obligations, do nothing, and live in the moment. Which explains why we spent more time in places that we liked (or where we hadn't eaten everything on the menu) or left sooner than planned when we found it too busy. We spent less time in the south because it was simply too hot. The freedom to pick up and head back to the cooler mountain temperatures is priceless.

Did we miss out on things as a result? Probably. But for us, luxury is not about seeking out the right, instagrammable place from a bucket list. We believe in simplicity and contentment. Living on a small surface, being nourished by nature's beauty. Where less is more and life is lived in the slow lane. Our mornings in all these stunning settings more or less followed the same ritual: getting the Bialetti going, taking a morning walk with Willy, reading up on the region, and making plans for the day. Drooling at the idea of all the specialities that we were going to taste that day.

Our camper-van trip through Italy ticked all our boxes and more. We followed our noses and gut to beautiful places and some of the best food we've had to date. As we headed home, we couldn't help but be overjoyed at the thought of seeing our kids again. At the same time, the idea of leaving this lovely country and its formidable food culture made us sad. Anyway, we still have lots of uncharted territory to explore. Plenty of reasons to go back, in other words!

BRAM'S JOURNEY

In the summer of 2022, I felt that the time had come to share my love for Italy with my three daughters Lena (11), Liv (9) and Loulou (5). My girlfriend Stephanie and I planned a three-week trip along Italy's west coast, with two major stops: Liguria in the north and the Amalfi Coast in the south. We rented a camper van for five, opting for a retro (near-old-timer) alcove camper. A beautifully kept classic camper van with not too much mileage on the odometer. We opted for cosiness and charm rather than the security and comfort of a newer model: our camper hit a maximum speed of 105 km/h when the wind was on our side and there was no airconditioning.

I love adventurous camper trips: discovering new places every day, deciding whether to leave or stay on a whim. Freedom! Happiness! But I wasn't travelling solo this time around and children don't like driving to different places every day. Their best travel memories are often made at campsites. To them, freedom means going to get an ice cream, playing with children who speak a different language, collecting stones... So we looked for and found a nice compromise, striking just the right balance between wanting to see a lot and a quiet family holiday with our children. We chose two campsites where we stayed for one week each: one in Rapallo to explore the Ligurian coast, and one in Sorrento, as a base for boat trips and excursions along the Amalfi Coast in the south. I had visited this beautiful region a few months earlier with my good friend Jelle, also known as The Messy Chef. Thankfully, I was aware that

the Amalfi Coast is virtually inaccessible when you're travelling in a camper.

As a family with children, we could have gone the easier route, because neither the Ligurian nor the Amalfi coast are known as beach holiday destinations. That is why finding good campsites with a swimming pool and a shop that sold ice creams was paramount. The two nice campsites that we had in mind did have one drawback: they did not accept advance bookings. Full is full of course, and as we all know, that can be quite tricky in regions with almost no alternatives. We rang them up one day in advance to check whether they still had a pitch for us and were in luck both times.

Both campsites were a hit and turned out to be perfectly suited as a base for lovely holidays in nice places with loads of delicious food. The campsite where we made a stopover in the middle of our journey, on Lake Bracciano, also was a stroke of luck. At the times the heat felt overpowering, especially in a camper without air conditioning, and our trip got off to an unfortunate false start (Stephanie's handbag was stolen while we were sleeping in our camper on a car park along a French motorway. Experienced campers will tell you that spending the night in one of these car parks is never a good idea and our experience confirms this). That said, our Italian summer was picture perfect, with lots of ice creams, lots of splashing in the pool, lots of breathtaking natural beauty, lots of "we need to come back", and plenty of time to relax together: *la dolce vita* at its best.

VENETO & LOMBARDIA

Cortina d'Ampezzo, Dolomiti

Lake Garda

Our trip through Italy starts in the north, on the border between South Tirol and the Veneto where the mountain peaks of the Dolomiti make for the most magnificent vistas. They are part of the Alps and are so beautiful and unique that they are even listed as Unesco World Heritage. In winter this is the place to be for skiers and snowboarders. In summer, hikers and adrenaline junkies flock here. In our case, our destination is a little further and lower. We are headed for Lake Garda, which is on the bucket list of many surfers because of its stunning location – nestled at the base of the Dolomite Mountains, bordering Lombardy. Don't be deterred by the fact that this is a tourist hotspot. All in all it's not that bad and the nature, the panoramas, and the Italian elegance more than make up for this. There are several romantic towns around Lake Garda, such as Malcesine, 'the pearl of Lake Garda'. The centre is busy, but in a good way, and car-free. The Veneto region extends southwards to the River Po, Italy's longest river. The lake and river are connected with each other by another river, the Mincio. Its banks are home to Valeggio sul Minco, among others, a picturesque, medieval town that is definitely worth the camper van detour.

— Cinque Torri

Le Corbusier declared the Dolomiti to be the most beautiful work of architecture in the world and who are we to disagree with one of the world's foremost architects? There's not much else you can do when you drive through and along the majestic rocks than gaze in awe at their amazing natural beauty. Especially at sunrise or sunset, when the mountains colour a delicate pink. This natural spectacle is called *enrosadira*. As you leave South Tirol behind you and head deeper into the Veneto, you can see the landscape change: pines make way for palm trees and chalets for the more typical Italian pink, yellow, and terracotta houses. The curtains in the windows dance just as energetically in the wind as the laundry on the line outside.

Mike always dreamt of surfing on Lake Garda. Non-surfers will also understand why because this place has all the ingredients for a great holiday. The towns around the lake are very touristy, especially in summer, but never at the detriment of the fun ambience. The lake's grandeur, the azure sky, and the mountains exceed anyone's expectations. If you don't mind spending the night close to other campers, you can easily find a nice pitch near the water without too much preparation. There are also lots of great restaurants with terraces on the lake. A leisurely stroll on the lake's banks after a great dinner: can you think of a better end to a hot summer's day?

Lake Garda

Valeggio sul Mincio

In the south, the Veneto borders on the Po plain. In recent years, this region has had to contend with extreme heat and draught. Some years, the situation is so bad that the immensely wide Po River runs dry even though the Mincio River, which starts from the southern tip of Lake Garda, flows into the Po. On the banks of the Mincio, you'll also find the lovely, picturesque town of Valeggio sul Mincio and the Ponte Visconteo over the river, which is a local attraction. We were blown away by the tortellini that we tasted in one of the nice waterside restaurants. A picture-perfect pit stop.

San Cassiano ⟶ ● ● ⟶ Cortina d'Ampezzo
Cinque Torri ⟶ ●

SOUTH TIROL

LOMBARDIA

VENETO

● ⟶ Malcesine

Lake Garda

● ⟶ Valeggio sul Mincio

Some more nice spots

Alta Badia is situated on the northern border of the Veneto, in the province of South Tirol and the heart of the Dolomiti. We definitely recommend this as your first stop if you are driving down from the north and are going on holiday in Italy. If you love pristine Alpine forests, pastoral meadows, and winding brooks, this is just the place for you. Or skiing, because from November to April, this is a ski resort. The walking trails that you can access in summer are among the best in Europe and the region is also famous for its culinary excellence, thanks to its regional cuisine and some award-winning (yes, even Michelin-starred) restaurants.

Camping Sass Dlacia is the highest campsite in the Dolomiti. The grounds are situated next to the Fanes-Sennes-Prags nature park, which has several hiking and cycling trails. But the campsite also has lots of assets for holidaymakers, including a spa. Despite the fact that we were there in summer, along with many other guests and campers, we found it very tranquil. It must look stunning during the winter months.
— Strada Sciarè 11, 39036 San Cassiano

Camping Cortina is located at the foot of some of the most beautiful mountains that Mother Nature has created, with pitches among the spruces. Wonderful! Additional charm points for the funky patterns on the toilet paper roll and the drying room above the sanitary facilities, for camping skiers (or skiing campers), who will be very happy that they have a place to air out their ski kit.
— Via Campo 2, 32043 Cortina d'Ampezzo

Camping Sass Dlacia

Camping Cortina

The **Cinque Torri** is a mountain range in the Dolomiti with, yes, five striking peaks. If you're nearby and you enjoy a good walk, then this is a top tip. There are various mapped looped trails, through valleys dotted with wildflowers, that take you past waterfalls, steep ridges (with breath-taking views) and even a fascinating historic site. During the First World War, Italian soldiers established their artillery headquarters and a defensive line here. Be prepared for the elevation gain and find some time for a pit stop – preferably with a refreshing beer in a mountain hut – to take in the magnificent surroundings.

The lovely, and therefore hugely popular, town of **Malcesine** is located on the eastern bank of Lake Garda. You can spend the night in your camper van on the lakeside campsite: while it is next to the motorway, the view of the water is amazing.

The new **Agricamping Maiella del Garda** is situated on the fringe of the lovely medieval town of Valeggio sul Mincio. This tiny farm campsite, with 15 pitches, is tucked between two motorways, which you can hear, but it didn't bother us. You receive a friendly, helpful welcome and it has lots of amenities, including a tiny pool.

—— Via Maiella Monti 1, 37067 Valeggio sul Mincio

—— Cinque Torri

Malcesine

FOOD

The first chapter of our culinary trip through Italy is dedicated to the border region between the three regions in the north: the Dolomites in South Tirol, Lombardy, and the Veneto. Mountain fare plays a prominent role in Northern Italian cuisine, with the menu including such filling, energy-rich dishes as ossobuco (veal shank stew), bresaola (dry-cured meat), as well as dumplings and schnitzel, two dishes in which you can taste the culinary influence of nearby Austria. Up north, the Italians tend to use lots of butter and cheese when they cook. If you use only the best ingredients, you don't need any extras to prepare a divine meal. We sampled pasta in butter sauce: so soft, so tender, so intensely satisfying. The cuisine of Lombardy and its capital Milan is rich and fulfilling too, featuring meat – thin slices of veal – cheese, butter and rice (risotto) as the main ingredients.

POLENTA WITH A POACHED EGG

Polenta. Either you love it (if you're in need of some comfort food) or you love to hate it. We like a creamier version, with loads of butter and cheese, and the runny yolk of the poached egg. So yummy!

Vegetarian option
Serves 4

4 eggs
splash of vinegar
1 l chicken stock or vegetable stock
150 g polenta
100 g Parmesan cheese
80 g dairy butter, plus a little extra
salt and pepper

Pour water and vinegar into a pot and bring to just below boiling point. Stir the water quickly in one direction until it's spinning around like a tornado. Break the egg into the centre. The swirling water will help the egg white to wrap around the yolk as it cooks. Using a slotted spoon, transfer the egg to a clean towel. Repeat for the other eggs.

Bring the stock to the boil, pour the polenta slowly into the liquid in a thin stream. Keep stirring until the polenta begins to set. Stir in the grated Parmesan cheese. Add the butter, combine, and season with salt and pepper.

Serve everyone a plate of steaming polenta with a poached egg.

CANEDERLI

**These bread dumplings are a good example of traditional mountain fare.
Any restaurant in a region with mountains and snowy winters will have bread dumplings
on the menu. They are served in soup or with some butter, but you can add all kinds
of other ingredients to them. They are quite bland in taste so they can do with a bit of flavour.
Use herbs like sage or a cheese that packs a punch like Gorgonzola.**

Vegetarian
Serves 3 to 4

500 g bread (preferably white bread)
125 ml whole milk
2 sprigs of sage
½ tbsp oregano
2 sprigs of flat-leaf parsley
½ onion
150 g Gorgonzola
2 eggs
2 tbsp 00 flour
30 g Parmesan cheese
dairy butter, to taste
1 tbsp olive oil
salt and pepper

Tear the bread into small pieces, place the bread in a large bowl with the milk. Soak for 30 minutes. Chop the herbs and dice the onion. Heat the oil in a pan and fry the onion.

Combine the fried onion, Gorgonzola, eggs, herbs, flour, salt, and pepper with the bread and knead well. Form the canederli (balls) and cook for 10 minutes in boiling water.

Heat the butter in a frying pan. Remove the canederli from the water and serve with the melted butter. Top with grated Parmesan cheese and season with black pepper.

PS
Italian 00 flour is a very finely milled flour and great for making a very elastic dough.

PS
We used dried oregano but if you can find fresh oregano, go for it: fresh is always better. But be sure to triple the amount: dried herbs are often more potent than fresh ones.

RISOTTO ALLA MILANESE

We briefly cross the border of the Veneto, into Lombardy, heading for Milan for this recipe. This is perhaps one of the most iconic Northern Italian dishes. In that case, we prefer to follow the traditional recipe without too much tweaking. There is a reason why this is a classic, after all. You could leave out the bone marrow, but we recommend that you don't as this imparts the rich taste. It doesn't get more comfort food than this. Grab a fork and eat it straight from the pan.

Serves 4

1 l beef stock
1 marrow bone
1 onion
80 g dairy butter
300 g risotto rice
    (arborio or carnaroli)
approx. 12 saffron strands
80 g Parmesan cheese
salt and pepper

Bring the beef stock to the boil and cook the beef bone for 15 minutes in the stock. Remove the beef bone from the stock and loosen the marrow from the bone.

Dice the onion. Melt half of the butter in a large deep pan and fry the onion until translucent. Add the marrow. Place the rice in the pan and stir until the rice is translucent. Pour in a ladleful of stock and let the rice absorb the stock, while stirring. Repeat until the rice is al dente.

Remove the pan from the heat and add the saffron. Carefully stir through the rest of the butter and the grated Parmesan cheese. Season with salt and pepper.

SCHIACCIATA WITH MUSHROOMS

Schiacciata is a pull-apart bread and is very similar to the better-known foccaccia. While they both are flatbreads, the more compact schiacciatina takes less time to rise and contains less water. If you can't find schiacciatina, foccaccia will do!

Serves 1 to 2

1 piece of pull-apart bread
2 slices pancetta
200 g wild mushrooms
2 sprigs of tarragon
1 tbsp mascarpone
1 tbsp olive oil
salt and pepper

Heat the oil in a pan and fry the pancetta. Remove from the pan and set aside.

Fry the mushrooms until golden brown in the same pan. Add some more olive oil if necessary. Season with salt and pepper. Pick the tarragon leaves off the sprig and add them to the mushrooms.

Cut open the bread and spread with the mascarpone. Arrange the mushrooms and the pancetta on the bread. Fold closed. Enjoy!

VITELLO ALLA MILANE∫E

Milan-style veal. The traditional recipe requires a tender veal cutlet – not the veal cutlet without the bone that we use in Belgium. A good cut of meat often doesn't need much more than some lemon juice and some fried capers. This dish is usually served with a side of spaghetti with tomato sauce. It also pairs nicely with a tomato salad.

Serves 4

100 g flour
2 eggs
100 g breadcrumbs
4 veal cutlets
100 g dairy butter
3 tbsp capers
3 sprigs of flat-leaf parsley
1½ lemon (juice and a wedge)
salt and pepper

Place the flour, the eggs, and the breadcrumbs in separate bowls. Beat the eggs with a fork. Dredge the meat in the flour, then the eggs, and finally the breadcrumbs.

Heat half of the butter in a frying pan and fry the meat over low heat until golden brown. Remove the meat from the pan. Melt the remaining butter in the pan to prepare the sauce.

Fry the capers over high heat in a splash of olive oil. Be careful, this can be quite messy and the oil may spit. Pour in the juice of 1 lemon. Season with salt and pepper.

Coarsely chop the parsley and toss it in the butter sauce. Pour the butter sauce over the meat. Season with salt and pepper and serve with a lemon wedge.

BRESAOLA

This typical Northern Italian dish is similar to carpaccio, but uses cured, dried lean beef. It takes just minutes to prepare – perfect for a quick lunch, as a snack or a starter. However, there's a but, simple dishes only work if your ingredients are of the highest quality. So use your best olive oil and your best balsamic vinegar – your best of everything, in fact.

Serves 4

rocket to taste
200 g bresaola
3 tbsp olive oil
2 tbsp balsamic vinegar
80 g Parmesan cheese
1 lemon (juice, optional)
salt and pepper

Arrange the rocket on a serving platter. Next, arrange the bresaola on the rocket leaves and drizzle with olive oil and balsamic vinegar. Sprinkle with the grated cheese and season with salt and pepper. If you like, sprinkle some lemon zest on top to add a little zingy kick.

LUMACHE

Lumache **are snails. In Northern Italy, nonnas love to cook snails with tomato and mushrooms but we prefer to keep things simple with some garlic butter and loads of herbs. A lovely treat.**

Approx. 40 snails

1 onion
1 garlic clove
2 sprigs of flat-leaf parsley
1 sprig of rosemary
1 tsp oregano
2 tbsp white wine
approx. 40 precooked snails
2 tbsp dairy butter
1 lemon (juice, optional)
2 tbsp olive oil
salt and pepper
bread for dipping

Finely chop the onion and the garlic. Heat the oil and the butter in a frying pan. Fry the onion and the garlic. Finely chop the herbs.

Add the snails to the frying pan. Fry for 5 minutes. Next, add the herbs and stir well. Pour the white wine into the pan and let the alcohol evaporate. Season with salt and pepper and drizzle with some lemon juice. Dip away!

PS
We used dried oregano but if you can find fresh oregano, go for it: fresh is always better. But be sure to triple the amount: dried herbs are often more potent than fresh ones.

OSSOBUCO

This is an Italian classic in which nothing can go wrong. All ossobuco needs is time and love. And if you ask us, it can also do with some gremolata – a mix of garlic, parsley, and lemon zest – which gives this dish the kick it needs.

Serves 4

4 veal shanks
5 to 6 tbsp flour
pinch of cayenne pepper
2 carrots
2 celery stalks
3 garlic cloves
3 sprigs of thyme
2 bay leaves
2 sprigs of sage
250 ml red wine
250 ml veal stock
300 g tinned tomatoes
½ bunch of flat-leaf parsley
1 lemon (zest)
3 tbsp olive oil
salt and pepper

Season the flour with salt, pepper, and cayenne pepper. Dredge the veal shanks in the seasoned flour. Heat the oil in a large frying pan, sear the meat on both sides and fry until golden brown. Remove from the pan and set aside.

Peel the carrots and wash the celery. Cut the vegetables into smaller pieces and cook in a casserole over low heat. Grate 2 garlic cloves. Add to the casserole, along with the thyme, the bay leaves, and the sage. Cook for 8 minutes.

Pour the red wine into the pan and let the alcohol evaporate. Now add the stock and the tomatoes. Crush the tomatoes. Stir well. Return the veal shanks to the casserole. Cover with a lid and simmer for 2 hours.

Prepare the gremolata: finely chop the parsley, place it in a bowl, add 1 grated garlic clove and the zest of one lemon. Mix well and serve the tender meat with the gremolata.

VALLE D'AOSTA & PIEMONTE

Monte Bianco

The nature of the Aosta Valley (Valle d'Aosta) is extraordinary. In fact, its beauty is such that our heart skipped not one but several beats as we drove through it. The mountains here, in the northwest of the country, are the place to go for long hikes, steep climbs, wild rivers, snow in summer, views that literally take your breath away, and delicious mountain fare with an Italian twist. The cherry on the cake? The Monte Bianco – or Mont Blanc as they call it in France. There are several pretty villages in the valley where you can unwind, including Brusson and Graines, Rhêmes-Saint-Georges, or Derby-Villaret and La Salle: all worth visiting, with their quaint chalets and spectacular setting, and a great place to set out on an amazing mountain hike. The contrast with Turin, in neighbouring Piemonte, is huge. This large city is definitely worth visiting if city trips are your thing, with lots of bars where you can find a place to sit on the terrace and watch city life file past, while enjoying the local specialities, which are often presented on a silver platter. The Barolo region is just an hour by car from Turin: heaven on earth for wine and nature lovers, with sleepy villages and hillsides covered with vines, where one of Italy's most precious grapes grow under the sun.

The mountains of the Aosta Valley served as a backdrop for *Le otto montagne*, Paolo Cognetti's bestseller about a beautiful friendship. In 2021, Felix Van Groeningen and Charlotte Vandermeersch pitched their tents in Graines (Brusson) to turn this novel into a film. Anyone who has seen the breathtaking footage will immediately understand how happy campers can be when they lean back in their chairs, in front of their camper van, on an idyllic campsite in this valley and gaze up at the magnificent mountains. Obviously, mountains like these are just begging to be climbed. Athletic visitors do this on foot but there are cable lifts to take you to the top. On a clear day, you can literally see forever. We felt humbled and moved, even brushing away a tear as we took in the amazing views.

Monte Bianco

Another highlight: our stay at a winery in the Barolo region, in the northwest of the hilly Le Langhe region. We parked our camper van under the fruit trees, among the hillside vineyards. Staying at a vintner means tasting the goods. Barolo is a powerhouse, the wine of kings. Like champagne, its appellation is protected, and several rules apply: Barolo can only be made from Nebbiolo grapes – an authentic grape variety from Piemonte –, which grow in the vineyards in one of eleven communes of the region. The minimum alcohol content is 13% and the wine must have aged for at least 38 months (including 18 months in oak or wood) before going to market. Then again: the result is something to write home about. We tasted, enjoyed, and bought wine.

Neive

We use the list of the most beautiful towns in Italy as our guide: *I borghi più belli d'Italia*. Many of them are picturesque, authentic towns, which also feel somewhat abandoned. In Piemonte, our list led us to medieval Neive. We found a terrace and ordered some of the local specialities, tasting more of the excellent local wines. In addition to being the cradle of Barolo, Piemonte is also known for its more accessible Barbera and noble Barbaresco wines.

Monte Bianco (Mont Blanc)
Courmayeur
Brusson
Graines
Rhêmes-Saint-Georges
VALLE D'AOSTA
Torredaniele
Settimo Vittone

Torino

PIEMONTE

Neive
La Morra

Some more nice spots

Camping Monte Bianco La Sorgente

Camping Monte Bianco La Sorgente is situated at the foot of Mont Blanc, on the Italian side of the renowned ski resort of Courmayeur. What a place! This is a popular destination for sports lovers and you can tell by looking at the guests: lots of hikers, cyclists and climbers. The campsite is also the starting point for many of the hiking trails through the mountains, past wild rivers, up steep mountain flanks and through Alpine pastures. The trail to Val Veny is especially stunning.

— Loc. Val Veny – Peuterey, 11013 Courmayeur

Camping Mombarone is a great place to camp if you intend to visit Turin. The campsite is situated along a road but there is a tiny river at the back of the site. The view is amazing, and they also have a pool. Go check it out!

— Fraz. Torredaniele 54, 10010 Settimo Vittone

Camping Mombarone

Turin

Time seems to have stopped in **Torredaniele**, a village between Valle d'Aosta and Turin. The streets are extremely steep but the walk past authentic houses, with lots of cheerfully coloured flowers in planters, is definitely rewarding.

Sleeping among the vines? Yes, you can at **La Rosa Nel Borgo**, a tiny agricampeggio in La Morra, which can accommodate just a few motorhomes or tents. The ambience is laidback and guests who are up for it are welcome to lend a hand in the vineyard: tending to the vines in spring or harvesting grapes in autumn. But nobody will blame you if you look on instead. Head to the wine cellars to sample some of the most delicious Barolo wines you've ever tasted!
— Via Roma 91, 12064 La Morra

Colourful **Cappella del Barolo** on the fringe of La Morra is a pleasant surprise. The chapel stands out among the vines, which belong to the Ceretto family. In 1999, they commissioned the renovation of the derelict building into a contemporary artwork. David Tremlett painted the interior decorations, Sol LeWitt's geometric exterior work in bold colours is also playful and lively.
— Strada Fontanazza, 12064 La Morra

Torredaniele

Cappella del Barolo

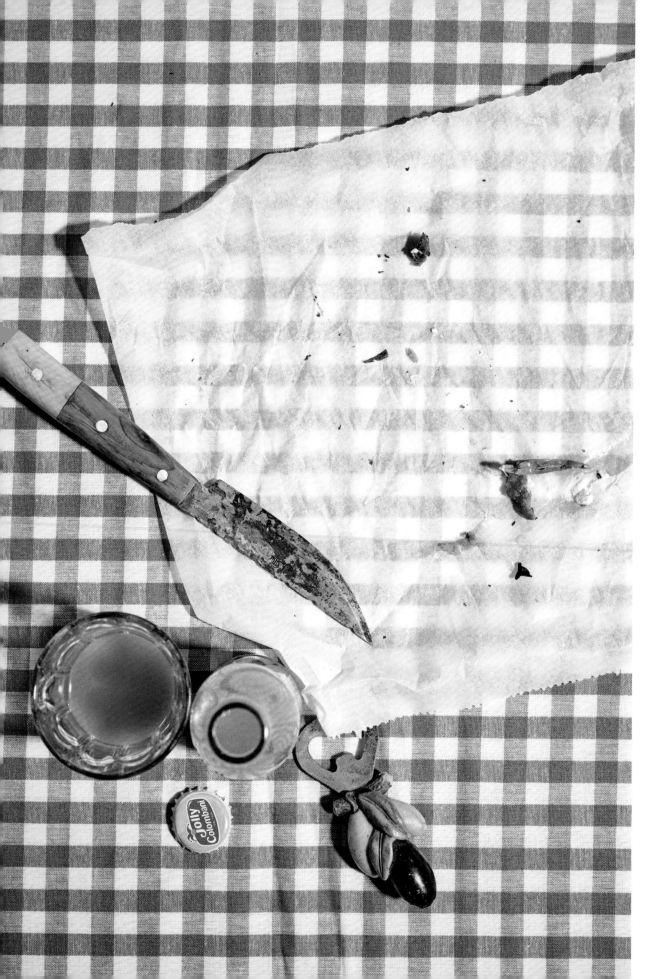

FOOD

Valle d'Aosta's geographical diversity is reflected in the dazzling array of products. The people here eat loads of polenta, bread, and soup and because the pastures are so well suited for grazing, this region also produces large amounts of dairy (sheep, cow and goat), including whole milk, butter, cream and cheese. The region's best-known cheese is fontina, which is made from cow's milk, and which connoisseurs agree is one of the best cheeses that Italy has to offer. Most people associate the culinary culture of neighbouring Piemonte with Barolo and hazelnuts – Nutella, the iconic chocolate hazelnut paste which most people know, conquered the world from the hills of Piemonte. But there's more! Besides Barolo, you should definitely sip some Barbaresco and Barbera when you visit the region. Excellent wines! Piemonte is also home to a wide range of cheeses and meats but the most precious ingredient in Piemontese cuisine has to be white truffle from Alba. A traditional speciality of the local *cucina povera* is bagna cauda, you can find our recipe on p. 69.

GNOCCHI

You can buy ready-made gnocchi anywhere, but they're actually very easy to make yourself. It takes some time and requires concentration, but that shouldn't be too much of a problem, when you're on holiday, right? We think it's a fun camping activity! You can buy special gnocchi boards to roll your gnocchi, but you don't really need to. Any worktop – the kitchen table at the campsite or your table outside of your camper van – and a potato press or a potato masher will do the trick.

Vegetarian
Serves 4

500 g floury potatoes
300 g 00 flour
some semolina flour
pinch of salt
150 g dairy butter
2 sprigs of sage
Parmesan or pecorino to taste
black pepper

Cook the potatoes in their jackets in salted boiling water. Drain and let the potatoes dry over heat. Peel the potatoes and mash or press them.

Dust your worktop with some 00 flour and combine the potato mash with the rest of the flour. Fold the dough to form a compact ball. Don't knead the dough like you would do for pasta or bread, because it develops the gluten, making the dough too stretchy. Shape small portions of the dough into long 'snakes'. Cut the snakes into small squares and press the tines of the fork into these pillowy squares.

Place the gnocchi on a plate or tray that you've dusted with semolina flour so they don't stick. Bring a pot of salted water to the boil, drop in the gnocchi, and cook for 4 minutes until they float to the top.

Mince half of the sage leaves. Melt some butter in a large frying pan and fry the whole sage leaves for 1 minute in the butter. Remove the leaves from the pan and add the rest of the butter. Once the butter has melted, you can add the sage. Season with salt and black pepper.

Toss the gnocchi in the savoury butter sauce and sprinkle with loads of Parmesan cheese or pecorino.

PS
Italian 00 flour is a very finely milled flour and great for making a very elastic dough.

PS
Semolina is a type of coarse flour that's made from durum wheat; it will add some extra bite.

PS
Once you've shaped the dough into squares, press the tines of a fork along the edges to make them jagged. This way your gnocchi will absorb the sauce better.

TONNATO SAUCE

We and our friends love vitello tonnato. You can get some finely sliced veal – the vitello – from the local butcher. They have the best quality so why bother to prepare it in your camper van? Making tonnato sauce yourself however is a good idea. It's not difficult and fresh sauce always tastes better. It pairs well with veal, or Romaine lettuce hearts, or chicken, or you can spread it on your sandwich.

Serves 4

25 ml cold veal stock
75 g tuna in spring water
2 anchovy fillets
1 hard-boiled egg
½ lemon (juice)
1 tbsp vinegar
pinch of sugar
salt and pepper
1 tbsp capers in sea salt

Place all the ingredients, except for the capers, in a measuring cup or bowl and mix. Add some water to loosen the texture.

Serve with veal and sprinkle with capers.

PANISSA

Risotto of Piemonte is prepared with Barolo wine, of course. Why should you use bad wine for cooking anyway? We have added some flavoursome pork fennel sausages to this panissa, as well as a few slices of guanciale. Pair it with a great-tasting Barolo and you have all the ingredients for a pleasant, cool summer evening.

Serves 4 to 6

300 g borlotti beans
2 shallots
2 celery stalks
50 g guanciale
4 fennel sausages
3 bay leaves
400 g Carnaroli rice
400 ml Barolo wine
1.2 l chicken stock
2 tbsp olive oil
2 tbsp dairy butter
curly parsley (optional)
Parmesan cheese (optional)

Drain the beans and rinse them under cold running water. Drain again and set aside.

Dice the shallots. Wash and finely slice the celery. Cut the guanciale into fine strips. Cut the sausages into equal parts.

Heat the oil in a large frying pan and fry the sausages until golden brown. Remove from the pan and set aside. Toss the shallots and the guanciale into the pan, along with the celery and the bay leaves, and cook for 8 minutes over low heat.

Add the rice and cook for 4 minutes. Pour the red wine into the pan and stir until the rice has absorbed it. Start adding the stock, a ladleful at a time.

When all the stock has been absorbed, you can add the beans and the sausages to the panissa. Once the rice is cooked and the panissa creamy, stir in some butter and serve immediately. You can garnish it with some parsley and grated Parmesan cheese.

PS
Guanciale is air-cured pork made from pig jowls.

CARNE CRUDA ALL'ALBESE

Who could have imagined that steak tartare is also a thing in Italy? No eggs or Worcestershire sauce though: we prefer it pure, with some great-tasting toppings – lemon and cheese – that deliver a flavour kick! We love them in equal measure and use them on everything. The lemon 'cooks' the meat slightly, similar to a ceviche.

Serves 4

a tender, lean beef cut (500 g)
1/2 lemon (juice)
1 garlic clove
a splash of good olive oil
coarse salt and black pepper

Toppings, to taste
shaved truffle or mushrooms
Parmesan cheese
rocket
parsley
grated lemon zest

Chop the meat with a sharp knife. Transfer the hand-cut mince to a mixing bowl and pour over the olive oil. Season with salt and pepper. Squeeze half of a lemon, grate 1 garlic clove and add.

Mix well and arrange the minced meat on the plates. Garnish with the toppings of your choice. Serve with a salad or bread.

INSALATA RUSSA

A Russian salad, in Italy? Yes indeed! You'll find this potato, vegetable, and egg salad on menus all over Italy. It's cheap and tasty, making it one of our favourite dishes when we go camping. This recipe is a real classic, and it is still taught in many Belgian catering schools. We use tuna for this Italian version, but the vegetarian alternative is just as good.

Vegetarian option
Serves 4 to 6

250 g waxy potatoes
150 g carrots
60 g (frozen) peas
100 g small gherkins
120 g tuna in olive oil
1 hard-boiled egg
2 to 3 tbsp mayonnaise
½ lemon
salt and pepper

Cook the potatoes in salty, boiling water until they are easily pierced. Drain and set aside to cool. Dice the potatoes. Peel the carrots, dice them, and cook them in salted, boiling water. Drain and set aside to cool.

Cut the gherkins into small pieces. Blanch the peas, then chill under cold, running water. Drain the tuna.

Combine gently, adding the mayonnaise – you can add more mayonnaise to taste. Season with salt and pepper and drizzle with the juice of half a lemon.

Serve on a dish or just put the bowl on the table. Cut the egg into wedges or slices and arrange on the salad. Eat with toast or any other good bread.

BAGNA CAUDA

The most addictive dip you'll ever come across! A lukewarm anchovy garlic dip with all the allure of a fondue – it may not sound that sexy but believe us when we say: oh boy. Remember, this delicacy is not French kiss-proof, unless you enjoy the dip together first, of course. Several other recipes exist but this is our riff on this popular dip.

Serves 4

50 g anchovy fillets
3 garlic cloves
75 ml olive oil
1 tbsp dairy butter
black pepper
4 tbsp full cream (optional)
raw and/or cooked vegetables
    of your choice, for dipping

Heat some olive oil in a frying pan, grate the garlic and add. Take care not to brown the garlic. Add the anchovies. Stir over low heat until the anchovies have dissolved. Pour in the rest of the olive oil and simmer for 20 minutes over very low heat.

Remove the saucepan from the heat and melt in the butter. If you want a milder-tasting dip, add cream. Leave out the cream if you like the full flavour of this dip. Season to taste with black pepper.

PS
Buy good quality anchovies. Fortunately, this is not that difficult in Italy!

PS
Endives, carrots, cucumber, cauliflower, fennel, radishes... Dip away with whatever you have in your fridge or any vegetables that are in season.

GIANDUJA

Hazelnuts, the true heart of Piemonte! We think hazelnuts are among the tastiest types of nuts, especially when combined with chocolate, another product that they are very proud of in Piemonte. (Whether theirs are better than the Belgian nuts? The proof is in the pudding, as they say). Gianduja is a hazelnut-chocolate (spreadable) paste – a luxurious Nutella if you like – that is often used as a filling in chocolates and as an ingredient in all kinds of desserts. Making cakes and cookies is not an option in the camper van, so we just make this paste instead. It's very tasty on a slice of bread or with an amaretti biscuit or as is, straight from the jar.

For 1 jar

80 g blanched hazelnuts
200 g dark chocolate
30 g sugar
pinch of salt
100 ml neutral vegetable oil

Toast the hazelnuts in a frying pan for 3 minutes. Finely chop them.

Melt the chocolate au bain marie. Add the sugar and the salt.
Stir in the oil and the finely chopped hazelnuts and pour into a jar.
It's that simple!

PS
Don't use butter as a substitute for the oil because the paste will congeal, and you won't be able to spread it on bread.

PS
Usually, you need a blender to make this spread but you can also finely chop the hazelnuts. The added crunch only adds to the taste.

PS
Store the paste in your cupboard so you can easily spread it.

LIGURIA

Rapallo

One of the smaller but at the same time nicer regions of Italy is Liguria, situated in the northwest, between Tuscany and the French border. It borders on the mountains to the east, on the sea to the west. The Ligurian coast is also called the Italian Riviera, and is a succession of postcard-worthy bays. We based ourselves in Rapallo, from where you can go on various day trips with public transport. Highly recommended because the most beautiful places are often difficult to reach with a camper van. The rocky coastal roads are often very tight and lined with endless bends. During our camper holiday with the children, we didn't make any city trips. A visit to Genoa, Liguria's capital, is still on our wish list. The port city has a fascinating history with periods of great wealth thanks to shipping and trade. It is built like an amphitheatre against the hills above the bay. A very imposing setting. Most people head for Cinque Terre in Liguria: a world-famous destination, consisting of five picturesque villages on cliffs and around bays. They are almost impossible to reach by camper although one of our stops, Il Poggio delle 5 Terre, is en route to the northernmost town of Monterosso. Booking is possible and highly recommended. From Rapallo you can also go to Cinque Terre by boat. We opted for another, wonderful boat trip along the coast, towards Portofino.

The waterfront of the tiny, but bustling town of Rapallo is a great place to get a good idea of the unique seaside ambience. On Thursdays, especially, because it's market day. The stalls sell anything and everything: food, household goods, Italian linens, and kitschy plastic, with the beach and the sea as a backdrop. We explored by bike which perhaps wasn't our brightest idea. There are almost no cycle paths, Italian traffic can be chaotic at best, and the inclines are often steep. Recommended: pasta in a local bistro or restaurant. The region's speciality is trofie al pesto alla Genovese (go to p. 88 for the recipe).

Rapallo

Liguria's Riviera has two parts. The Riviera di Ponente extends to the west of Genoa, with wide beaches. We visited the eastern part, the Riviera di Levante, with its rugged rocks. The ideal way to explore this amazing coastline is by boat. We took the ferry to Portofino. There are several departures every hour and you buy your ticket on the spot from the ticket office. Our boat stopped at Santa Margherita, Portofino, and San Fruttuoso; they are all just 15 minutes from each other. From the water, you can see how breathtaking the Ligurian coast is, with countless inlets and small bays such as Baia del Silenzio, and small towns that dot the rocky hillsides. If you have the time, head for San Fruttuoso, a hamlet with just a few residents and cliffs that are up to 40 metres high.

Arriving at Portofino by boat is an amazing experience. The – over the top – luxury yachts that are moored here, as well as the beautiful historic Villa Beatrice that sits high on a cliff, are an indication that this is not a tranquil fishing village but an upscale resort. Since the 1950s, this has been the Saint Tropez of Italy, a popular holiday destination for the jet set. The famous and the rich come here to see and be seen. Don't expect to find souvenir shops near the marina, instead the shops sell brands like Rolex and Chanel. And yet, the town has managed to retain its picturesque character and the natural setting, on a spit among the cliffs, is never boring.

Portofino

You can also admire the rocky coastline between
Rapallo and Portofino from onland. We took the
bus to the bay of Paraggi, but there's also a fun
coastal path for hikers. En route, you'll run into
idyllic *spiaggi pubblici* or public beaches.
Many of them are just an inlet, with some sand,
but sometimes that's all you need to be happy …

LIGURIA

●—— Genova

●—— Rapallo

San Fruttuoso ——● ● ●——— Paraggi

●—— Portofino

Some more nice spots

During the high season, the tiny **Camping Rapallo** does not accept bookings. If you want to be sure of a pitch here, you'll need to get lucky. But the pitches are more than worth of it, because the surroundings are beautiful, and the olive trees provide lots of shade – something you'll definitely appreciate on summer days in Italy. The campsite also has a swimming pool, which is always a hit with children. While they don't have a restaurant proper, they light the wood-fired oven every evening, serving droolworthy pizzas. The kids' pizzas even come with fries!

●— Via San Lazzaro 4/d, 16035 Rapallo

The interior of **La Tana Dell'Orso** in Rapallo is reminiscent of a redone kebab shop. The menu is a printed sheet, featuring six dishes which are prepared fresh in-house. If you believe in appearances, you'll probably head elsewhere. And that would be a mistake because we ate the best meal of our holiday here: an amazing pasta frutti di mare, and the chef's speciality, a ragù mixed with pesto. So simple and prepared with such passion and skill by the owner. His wife and children run the front of house. This is a real family business. And the bill was surprisingly cheap!

●— Via Santa Maria del Campo 111, 16035 Rapallo

A large stretch of the beach between Portofino and nearby **Baia di Paraggi** is operated by hotels. This means you must pay for a lounger and an umbrella. The tiny public beaches are usually heaving with people. While a lounger on a private beach may not be cheap, it does come with privacy to change, fresh towels, and service. In the bay at Paraggi, we found a nice place where we treated ourselves to this luxury: watching your children play in the sand and the water in a picturesque bay, while sipping a glass of rosé... Life doesn't get much better than this.

●— Camping Rapallo

FOOD

Liguria's cuisine is light, simple and rich in taste, thanks to the Mediterranean climate and the fertile soil. Many Ligurian dishes are best eaten in summer, making them a great choice for camper holidays. Here the culinary tradition has more foreign influences than elsewhere in Italy, largely thanks to the port of the capital city, Genoa: through the ages, ingredients from all over the world have found their way from overseas to the docks of Genoa. The stockfish on the next pages is a good example of this. Liguria's hills provide just the right habitat for herbs like thyme, sage, rosemary, oregano, and basil, which grow everywhere you look among the shrubs. Pesto, widely popular nowadays, originally hails from Liguria; some cities here have their own local variant with local herbs and nuts. And connoisseurs say that the olive oil from Liguria is the best you'll find in Italy.

TROFIE AL PESTO GENOVESE

Pesto Genovese is another popular staple of Italian cuisine. For really tasty, good pesto, you'll need a mortar and pestle, and good quality ingredients. We don't believe in blending, mixing, or chopping anything for this recipe. In Liguria, this green pesto is traditionally served as an uncooked cold sauce with trofie, the thin twisted pasta of this region.

Vegetarian
Serves 4

For the pesto
1 garlic clove
50 g basil
3 tbsp pine nuts
4 tbsp Parmesan cheese
4 tbsp olive oil (extra virgin)
pinch of salt

Other ingredients
500 g trofie
rocket to taste
4 tbsp toasted pine nuts
black pepper

Pound the garlic and salt to a paste, using a mortar and pestle. Add the pine nuts, the basil and the grated cheese, and continue to crush them with the pestle, smashing and grinding them, until a sticky paste forms. Slowly drizzle in the olive oil.

Cook the pasta in salted, boiling water until al dente. Remove the pasta from the water and toss with the pesto. Garnish with the toasted pine nuts and some rocket. Season with salt and pepper.

RISOTTO WITH HAZELNUT PESTO

Obviously, you can make pesto from lots of other nuts and herbs. And you don't necessarily need to serve it with pasta as this tasty risotto recipe proves.

Vegetarian
Serves 4

For the pesto
1 garlic clove
50 g rocket
3 tbsp toasted hazelnuts
4 tbsp Parmesan cheese
4 tbsp olive oil (extra virgin)
pinch of salt

For the risotto
200 g cherry vine tomatoes
2 onions
1 garlic clove
200 g risotto rice
    (arborio or carnaroli)
1½ l vegetable stock
2 tbsp dairy butter
50 g Parmesan cheese
40 g roasted hazelnuts
2 tbsp olive oil + extra for serving
salt and pepper

Follow the recipe on p. 88 to prepare the pesto but substitute the pine nuts with toasted hazelnuts and the basil with rocket.

Heat a splash of olive oil in a small frying pan and fry the cherry tomatoes until tender. Season with salt and pepper and set aside. Coarsely chop the roasted hazelnuts.

Finely chop the onion and the garlic. Heat 2 tbsp of oil in a large frying pan and fry the garlic and the onion until translucent. Add the rice, cook for 2 minutes. Gradually pour in the vegetable stock while stirring continuously. Wait until the rice has absorbed the stock before adding another ladleful. Make sure the rice is creamy. Season with salt and pepper.

Remove the pan from the heat and stir in the butter. Next, stir in the grated cheese, and then the pesto. Garnish with the toasted hazelnuts and the fried tomatoes.

FARINATA DI CECI WITH RICOTTA

This thin Italian pancake, made of chickpea flour, hails from the coastal region of Liguria. It's very similar to pizza, meaning you can add any savoury toppings you want. Traditionally, the dough (like pizza) is cooked in an oven, but you can also prepare your farinata on a plancha or in an ovenproof pan on your barbecue under a closed lid.

Vegetarian
Serves 2

For the batter
100 g chickpea flour
300 ml water
2 sprigs of rosemary
1 tbsp oregano
pinch of chilli powder
1 garlic clove
3 tbsp + 2 tbsp olive oil

For the topping
1 courgette
½ sweet onion
2 tbsp ricotta
½ lemon (zest)
small bunch of rocket leaves
oregano
pinch of cayenne pepper

Chop the herbs. Combine all the ingredients (except the garlic) for the batter; also keep 2 tbsp olive oil for frying. Grate the garlic and add. Let the batter rest for at least one hour.

Wash and slice the courgette into thin slices and grill on both sides. Peel and cut the onion into half-moons. Heat a frying pan until very hot. Pour in the olive oil. Pour a thin layer of the batter into the pan and bake for about 10 to 15 minutes in a closed barbecue at a high temperature until set.

Remove the farinata from the barbecue and spread some ricotta on it. Arrange the courgette slices, rocket, and onion on top of it. Season with salt and pepper, oregano, and a pinch of cayenne pepper.

PS
We used dried oregano but if you can find fresh oregano, go for it: fresh is always better. But be sure to triple the amount: dried herbs are often more potent than fresh ones.

ARTICHOKE WITH TAPENADE

A delightful, light snack that isn't too filling. A great idea for aperitivo and easy to eat: the perfect accompaniment to meaningful conversations!

Vegetarian
Serves 4 as an appetizer

1 artichoke
1 lemon (zest and juice)
10 pepper corns
1 sprig of rosemary
1 bay leaf
1 onion
2 tbsp olive tapenade
Parmesan cheese
parsley
pinch of salt

Place the artichoke in a casserole and fill with water until the artichoke is fully submerged. Add the lemon peel to the water, along with the peppercorns, the rosemary, the bay leaf, and a pinch of salt. Peel and halve the onion. Add it to the casserole. Cook the artichoke for 40 minutes over low heat. Drain.

Coarsely chop the parsley. Cut the artichoke in half and spread the olive tapenade on the artichoke halves. Sprinkle with some grated Parmesan cheese, garnish with parsley. Drizzle some lemon juice over the artichokes and you're good to go.

STOCCAFISSO ALLA GENOVESE

Stoccafisso is Italian for stockfish: dried cod, a product that you'd typically expect to find in Scandinavia. But it's also a popular ingredient in Italian cuisine since the 15th century when a Venetian merchant went off course and ended up in Norway. After tasting the stockfish, he promptly loaded up his ship with tons of this good stuff to bring back to Italy. In Genoa, they serve stockfish in a stew, with olives and pine nuts. The Genoese usually add dried wild mushrooms, but we prefer to leave them out.

Serves 4

800 g soaked stockfish
1 onion
3 garlic cloves
1 celery stalk
1 carrot
3 anchovy fillets
500 g waxy potatoes
400 g peeled tomatoes
1 glass white wine
70 g toasted pine nuts
100 g black olives
parsley
3 tbsp olive oil

Clean the stockfish and cut into serving portions.

Finely chop the onion and the garlic. Wash the celery, clean it, and cut it into small pieces. Peel the carrot and cut it into small pieces. Heat the oil in a deep frying pan and fry the onion and the garlic until translucent, with the anchovy fillets. Add the carrot and the celery and cook for 5 minutes.

Peel and cut the potatoes into equal pieces. Add the stockfish, the potatoes, and the tomatoes to the pan. Pour in the white wine. Stir well and simmer until the potatoes are easily pierced with a fork. Add some water if necessary.

When everything is cooked through, add the toasted pine nuts and the olives to the stew. Season with salt and pepper. Garnish with some parsley.

CONIGLIO ALLA LIGURE

We don't like to admit it but, in our opinion, this Italian recipe for rabbit is better than the Belgian version with prunes. The delicious Taggiasca olives in this recipe add a burst of flavour. Add pine nuts to this tantalising mix and you'll soon realise how all these flavours are perfectly balanced. This dish ticks all the boxes!

Serves 4

1½ kg rabbit, cut up in pieces
1 onion
2 garlic cloves
1 carrot
1 glass red wine
2 cloves
2 bay leaves
2 sprigs of rosemary
250 ml beef stock
400 g waxy potatoes
100 g Taggiasca olives
80 g toasted pine nuts
½ lemon (juice)
parsley
3 tbsp olive oil
salt and pepper

Finely chop the onion and the garlic. Peel the carrot and dice it. Heat the oil in a casserole and fry the garlic, the onion, and the carrot. Place the rabbit pieces in the casserole and sear. Pour the wine into the casserole and let the alcohol evaporate.

Add the cloves, the bay leaves, and the rosemary to the casserole, along with the stock. Simmer for 30 minutes.

Peel the potatoes and quarter them. Add the potatoes, the olives, and the pine nuts to the casserole. Simmer for another 30 minutes. Add some stock if your stew looks too dry. Season with salt and pepper and drizzle with some lemon juice. Garnish with some parsley.

MARINATED OLIVES

A great snack to have on hand. Buy different types of olives from the local shops or markets and get marinating.

Serves 2 for 3 days, or share with
your campsite neighbours

500 g olives of your choice
2 lemons
2 oranges
2 garlic cloves
1 anchovy
½ bunch of flat-leaf parsley (optional)
200 ml olive oil (extra virgin)
black pepper

Peel the lemons and one orange (make sure the peels are thin) and squeeze for the juice. Slice the other orange.

Place the olives in a bowl, pour over the lemon juice and the olive oil. Press the garlic and add. Finely slice the anchovies and combine with the olives. Season with pepper. Garnish with some parsley if you want.

EMILIA-ROMAGNA

Countryside near Bologna

Bologna

Emilia-Romagna is known as Italy's belly, not because of its location (in the north, straddling Italy's thigh) but because it boasts some of the country's most famous products. This is a very fertile region, with lots of agriculture, grape production (obviously), and livestock rearing. The place to sample such delicious regional products as Parma ham, egg pasta, Parmesan cheese and aceto balsamico di Modena. We think that you should really follow your nose if you're visiting this region. So stop into one of the divine food shops in Parma, where you can taste the most delicious prosciutto, or find a table on a terrace in Bologna and order a mouth-wateringly good porchetta sandwich and a charcuterie board with mortadella. If possible, and temperatures permitting, try to combine it with a visit to a city because Bologna – the largest city in Emilia-Romagna – especially is definitely worth visiting. But as is so often the case in Italy, the most extraordinary culinary experiences are found outside the city limits. Or better yet, you just happen upon them. Before you know it, you'll be invited to tuck into a meal on a farm in the hills around Bologna where the hostess is such a good cook that you'll never forget that one plate of lasagne that she served you that night…

Bologna: what a city! Such beauty, such grandeur. If you're into art, architecture, or culture, then look no further. The two most prominent symbols of the city are the medieval towers. And surely you'll be blown away by the impressive Cathedral of San Pietro and the Piazza Maggiore. Food lovers will have to head elsewhere for the city's most beautiful culinary treasures, more specifically in the windows of the many food shops which are stacked with dozens of different types of tortellini, mortadella, glistening slices of porchetta, and bread. The city is dotted with authentic places to eat and at certain times of the day you get to experience the typically lively ambience of an Italian city.

Agricamper Italia (see p. 8) will take you to some unique places, such as a farm in the hilly countryside around Bologna, with a view of the vineyards, horses, and fruit orchards. The farmer asks that guests park their camper vans in the car park so the animals are not disturbed. But he more than makes up for this with the amazing meal to which he treats his guests, starting with the bottle of red house wine which he uncorks. It doesn't have a label, instead he has drawn a camper van on the bottle with a marker. It's all so charming and authentic (and the wine is sooo good) that you know that you're in for a fantastic evening. Next up, a plate of prosciutto, porchetta, and fried pasta (crescentine). And the best is yet to come: a plate of steaming lasagne which tastes unlike any lasagne you've ever had, the kind of ragù that melts in your mouth with incredible flavour, and ravioli that are so creamy, tender and decadent ... There are no words to explain it. Definitely one of our more memorable culinary experiences!

Agriturismo La Concia

Parma

EMILIA-ROMAGNA

Bologna

Monzuno

Pennabilli

Some more nice spots

— Camping Le Querce

Parma has tons of food shops that sell anything from fresh meat and pasta to local, artisanal products. We stopped at **La Rocca di Silvano Romani** and ended up buying some exquisite-tasting Prosciutto di San Daniele, a large chunk of incredibly good Parmesan cheese, balsamic vinegar from Giuseppe Giusti (our favourite, striking just the right balance between sweetness and acidity, not too cloying and not too runny) and even Culatello di Zibello, a noble and very exclusive ham. It's fair to say that we felt like kids in a toy shop.
— Via Marco Emilio Lepido 1/c, 43123 Parma

A handy stop on the road from Bologna to Firenze is **Camping Le Querce**. *Querce* is Italian for oak trees, one of the assets of this campsite. Everywhere you look, tall oak trees provide shade and privacy. The campsite has a pool, which is definitely a plus given the Italian climate.
— Strada Provinciale 61, 40036 Monzuno

Agriturismo La Concia is located in the hills above Pennabilli in the Province of Rimini where Emilia-Romagna borders on Le Marche and Tuscany. A stunning place that is postcard and Instagram-worthy: a nice, cosy pool with picturesque orange canopies, a stunning view (at sunset especially), peace and quiet, trees and a restaurant with a terrace under the vines. The father of the family welcomes you and assigns you your pitch. We loved it so much here that we stayed longer than planned: it's very difficult to leave when you've found the perfect place to relax and do absolutely nothing!
— Via Ca' Berbece 13, 47864 Pennabilli

— Agriturismo La Concia

FOOD

Many iconic Italian delicacies originated in Emilia-Romagna, starting with ragù alla Bolognese, a traditional 19th-century recipe, made with minced beef, pancetta, onion, and tomatoes. Note that this sauce has nothing to do with the popular bastardised version that you'll find on so many menus outside of Italy. Cheese with ragù is a big no by the way, even though Emilia-Romagna is famous for its delicious Parmigiano Reggiano cheese. Modena is the home of balsamic vinegar, while Parma ham comes from – yes, you guessed it – Parma. Did you know that they make an even tastier, refined ham, called Culatello, in the north of the Province of Parma? This superb quality meat from smaller, black pigs, such as the Nero di Parma or Mora Romagnola, spends 1½ to 3 years ageing in dark cellars, with natural ventilation and mist. Because it's such a small-scale production, Culatello is rare and in demand, with part of the production going to King Charles and other royals. If you happen to spot some, buy it! The same applies to many of the delicacies that you can buy from farm stands, including cheese, jam, or tomatoes and even fresh ragù, which the farmer's wife has scooped into jars for you to take home.

PIADINA ROMAGNOLA WITH MORTADELLA

Pure, unadulterated street food! This is an easy recipe for the typically Italian piadina flatbreads. You'll need just a few ingredients and it's very satisfying to make. We tend to fill them with mortadella and mozzarella, but obviously you're free to use whatever's in your fridge. A sweet filling also works well, like the chocolate spread in this book (p. 70).

For 6 piadina wraps

500 g 00 flour
1 tbsp baking soda
125 g oil
pinch of salt
170 g water

For the filling
6 tsp red pesto
6 slices mortadella
3 fresh mozzarella balls
small bunch of rocket leaves
Parmesan cheese
oregano
chilli flakes
balsamic vinegar

Place the flour, the baking soda, the oil, and the salt in a large bowl and mix well. Gradually add the water and knead to obtain a compact, homogeneous dough. Form a ball, cover, and let rest for 30 minutes.

Remove the dough from the bowl and roll into a 'snake'. Divide the snake into 6 portions and roll into 6 small balls. Cover and let the dough rest for 30 minutes.

Roll out each dough ball to form a flatbread. Cook the piadinas one at a time in a preheated pan, for 2 minutes per side.

Spread the red pesto on your piadina and add mozzarella, mortadella, and rocket. Drizzle with balsamic vinegar, and sprinkle with oregano, grated Parmesan cheese, and chilli flakes.

PS
00 flour is very finely milled Italian (durum wheat) flour.

RICOTTA AND ſPINACH TORTELLI

This book wouldn't be complete with at least one recipe for home-made pasta, right? We chose tortelli for personal, nostalgic reasons. As a young family, we always had tortelli on hand to whip up some dinner presto to fill our kids' bellies.

Vegetarian
Serves 4 to 6

For the pasta
400 g 00 flour
4 eggs
additional flour for dusting

For the filling
180 g spinach
1 garlic clove
pinch of nutmeg
550 g ricotta
1 tbsp olive oil
salt and pepper

To finish
50 g butter
50 g Parmesan cheese
black pepper

PS
Gluten is formed during kneading, causing the dough to become more elastic.

Place the flour on your worktop or table and make a well in the centre. Gently pour the eggs into the well and use a fork to whisk them. Incorporate the flour little by little and break up any clumps with the fork. Repeat to form a compact dough.

Briefly knead the dough and scrape any remaining flour from your worktop. The dough must feel smooth and not sticky: feel free to add some flour. Now you knead the dough for at least 10 minutes. Put the dough in a bowl, cover, and let it rest for at least 30 minutes.

Make the filling: heat the oil in a frying pan and cook the spinach briefly. Grate the garlic and add. Season with salt, pepper, and nutmeg. Drain the spinach well.

Cut the dough into 4 equal pieces roll each piece out into a strip of approx. 10 cm wide. Dust with flour. Combine the spinach with the ricotta. Spoon the filling onto the strips of pasta in a straight line, 5 cm apart. Cover the filling with another strip of pasta and press down around the filling. Use a pasta cutter to trim your tortelli on all sides into squares.

Cook the tortelli for 4 minutes in salted, boiling water. Melt the butter in a small frying pan and add a ladleful of the pasta water. Serve the tortelli in a bowl with the butter sauce and garnish with some grated Parmesan cheese. Season with more black pepper.

OUR ONE AND ONLY RAGÙ

This recipe has been a long in the time making, with lots of trials and experiments. We are really happy with it, which is why we have chosen to include in this book. To be fair, you can't improve or tweak such a classic dish as a non-Italian. In principle, only real Italian mammas, pappas, nonnas and nonnos can do this because in Italy each family has its own tried and tested recipe. We hope you enjoy ours...

Serves 4 hungry eaters

1 onion
3 carrots
3 celery stalks
100 g pancetta
600 g ribeye
200 g veal fillet
3 tbsp tomato purée
2 garlic cloves
2 bay leaves
130 ml good red wine
500 ml beef stock
4 tbsp olive oil
salt and pepper
400 g pasta

Dice the onion. Wash the celery and cut it into small pieces. Peel the carrots and cut them into small pieces. Heat the oil in a large deep frying pan. Fry the vegetables for 15 minutes over low heat.

Finely chop the ribeye and the veal and cut the pancetta into small pieces.

Toss the pancetta with the vegetables and fry for a few minutes. Add the tomato purée and cook for another 5 minutes.

Add the meat to the vegetables and turn up the heat. If necessary, add some olive oil. Fry the meat until tender and crispy. Grate the garlic. Add the garlic and the bay leaves to the meat. Pour the wine into the pan and let the alcohol evaporate.

Next, pour in the stock and bring to a simmer. Then turn it down so it's bubbling. Cover and cook for 3 hours. Stir now and again and add some stock if your ragù looks dry. Season with salt and pepper.

Cook the pasta in salted, boiling water. Add the pasta to the ragù and add a generous ladle of the pasta water. Stir well so the ragù coats the pasta nicely. Serve immediately.

FRIGGIONE BOLOGNESE

A sweet onion and tomato salsa, that's all. But don't be fooled by how simple this recipe looks. This is a proper flavour bomb! Time is the essential magical ingredient. We recommend making this salsa one day ahead. Admittedly this is not the easiest dish to be preparing in a camper van but we really wanted to share it with you. Do you have a campfire? Use it to avoid using gas in your camper van. Or make your salsa at home and enjoy it on the road.

Vegetarian
Serves 4

4 sweet onions
1 tsp sugar
1 tsp salt
1 tin of the best quality tomatoes
    (e.g., Mutti) or 5 fresh, peeled tomatoes
pepper
bread
cheese to taste

Peel and cut the onions into half-moons. Combine the onions with the salt and the sugar in a mixing bowl. Massage well. Macerate for at least 4 hours.

Heat the oil in a pan and braise the onions with the liquid of the maceration for at least 2 hours over low heat until brown. The mixture must have a creamy consistency. Add the peeled tomatoes and simmer for another 2 hours.

Season with pepper and serve with bread - preferably bruschetta - and (melted) cheese.

ANTIPASTI

A traditional Italian antipasti platter is a great example of how the whole is greater than the sum of its parts. Choose only the best ingredients, which happen to be widely available in Italy. Look for local, independent traders in villages: talk to the cheesemaker, visit the butcher who is renowned for his excellent mortadella, take some time to find the best porchetta... Taste and buy what you like, as long as it's fresh, and produced locally.

Serves 4, for aperitivo

60 g fresh ricotta
2 anchovy fillets
1 lemon (zest)
mortadella
pecorino
chargrilled marinated vegetables
    such as artichokes, courgette, aubergine ...
baked black olives
prosciutto
breadsticks (grissini)
fennel biscuits (taralli)
balsamic vinegar
1 tbsp olive oil
pepper

Place the ricotta on a small platter and arrange the anchovy fillets on top of it. Sprinkle with some lemon zest, season with pepper, and drizzle with olive oil.

Arrange the remaining ingredients on a wooden board and drizzle some balsamic vinegar over the pecorino. Pour everyone a nice drink and enjoy.

VANILLA ICE CREAM WITH BALSAMIC VINEGAR

Come again? Vanilla ice cream with balsamic vinegar? Yup, the light, sweet and sour of the right aceto balsamico works a charm when combined with vanilla ice cream. Add some crunch for a fantastic, surprising dessert which takes just minutes to prepare. Don't have a freezer in your camper? Your campsite should have one.

Vegetarian
Serves 2

4 scoops vanilla ice cream
4 amaretti biscuits
handful of pistachios
splash of good quality balsamic vinegar

Coarsely chop the pistachios and crumble the amaretti. Scoop the ice cream into bowls or glasses. Sprinkle with the nuts and the biscuits. Drizzle with some balsamic vinegar.

PIT STOP: TOSCANA

Magnificent Tuscany needs no introduction! A popular destination with many Belgian and Dutch holidaymakers, Tuscany and its rolling, hillside vineyards, magnificent culture cities, and excellent wines never disappoints. It's also paradise for campers because many wineries have set up great pitches for camper vans on their land.

We booked a pitch at the **Luxor Chianti** glamping in Castellina in Chianti, which comes with lots of bonus features: nice pitches under the trees, a swimming pool, and a bar. We visited a small winery near Castellara di Castellina, where we tasted some amazing Chianti, buying some to take home.
—— Località Trasqua, 53011 Castellina in Chianti

Art and architecture lovers are spoilt for choice in Tuscany: Firenze, Lucca, Volterra, Montepulciano... The dazzling array of heritage in these cities is simply incredible. We headed to **Siena**. Tip: park your car or camper van on the city fringe and take the tram into the historic city centre, where you can visit the Duomo, a stunning example of Italian Gothic architecture, with a unique, beautifully decorated façade. The shell-shaped Piazza del Campo with its 'Fountain of Joy' is another must-see. Definitely one of Europe's most beautiful medieval town squares.

—— Castellina in Chianti

Monteriggioni

Castellina in Chianti

Siena

LE MARCHE

The hilly region of Le Marche is really the green heart of Italy, and is situated between the Apennines and the Adriatic, alongside Umbria and Tuscany. It's just as beautiful as the other top tourist destinations, but not as busy, especially if you head land inwards. The crowds get bigger in August when the campsites are full of Italians who are on their summer holiday. They prefer Le Marche and we agree! It's also a great destination if you're a cycling fan, or so we were reliably informed by one of our friends who's a bit of a sports fanatic. This also happens to be Marco 'Il Elefantino' Pantani's region! In terms of culture and heritage, Le Marche also has lots to offer, with rolling hills and beautiful villages, where even the tiniest churches are full of art and treasures just waiting to be discovered. Our recommendation: every time you walk past a church in Italy, go in and let the beauty and tranquillity wash over you. Even if you're looking to beat the heat on a sunny day – because temperatures do soar in Le Marche! – or to light a candle for someone you love or or who needs it. You can also cool off on the beaches of Le Marche, although the water can be disappointingly warm when there's no wind.

Torre di Palme

Pesaro

Anyone who travels through Italy with a list of
the most beautiful medieval towns *(I borghi più
belli d'Italia)* as a guideline will be able to tick
off several must-sees in Le Marche. The narrow
alleys are both picturesque and refreshingly cool
because the sun never shines there. The medieval
people who built these villages knew exactly
what they were doing. Churches and coffee
are always something we look forward to when
visiting a town. Always good, always strong:
can you think of anything better than a freshly
brewed espresso from a local bar?

Le Marche's most popular and liveliest seaside resort is Pesaro – which has a railway station and that explains why so many Italians come here to relax. It's a great place for surfing but finding a place to sit on the beach can be quite challenging because it does get very busy. Then again, the view of the waves at sunset is so gorgeous that you forget everything and everyone around you. Finding a nice campsite here is not exactly easy: most of them are situated very close to each other, and the same applies to the pitches: in very close proximity to each other, Italian style.

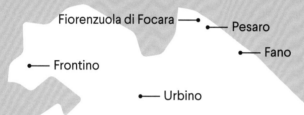

Fiorenzuola di Focara —●

Pesaro ●—

Fano ●—

Frontino ●—

Urbino ●—

LE MARCHE

—● Torre di Palme

Some more nice spots

The lovely village of **Frontino** (population: 285) has tons of medieval charm and is a great place for a stroll through picturesque squares and quiet streets.

Apparently, **Urbino** is one of the best-preserved Renaissance cities in Italy. Raphael, the 'prince of painters', was born here in 1483 and is widely considered one of the most important representatives of this art movement. You can see many of his works in Vatican City. Urbino is also home to one of Italy's oldest universities, which was founded in the 16th century. An artful and vibrant city, in other words, with a student population of 25,000.

Frontino

The medieval town of **Torre di Palme** is close to the coast and is – obviously – included on our list of most beautiful towns. This relatively unknown gem also has a lot of stunning Renaissance architecture in store for you.

There are very few nice campsites in Pesaro proper. We spent one night at **Sosta Camper Il Rospo**, which to be honest is not much more than a car park next to a restaurant, although the view through the fence is amazing. We were the only visitors but come August, we think it may be much busier.

●— Strada Nazionale Adriatica Nord 43/b, 61032 Fano

We stopped near Pesaro, staying at **Camping Panorama**, near Parco Naturale Monte San Bartolo, which is surrounded by cliffs, the sea, wineries and country estates. Its location is a real bonus as was the charming – downright flirty – man who welcomed us and assigned us a pitch. Unfortunately, the pitch was less than ideal for our large camper van. You need to walk a bit to see the sea and the restaurant wasn't that great, but the swimming pool will more than make up for this.

●— Strada Brisighella 7/c, 61121 Fiorenzuola di Focara

●— Torre di Palme

FOOD

The cuisine of Le Marche is just as diverse as the region's landscape. Fresh fish and seafood dominate the menu in the eastern coastal areas, making way for game in the mountainous west. The fertile land in the centre of the region is used to grow wheat and olives, and rear fowl and livestock. In Le Marche, each province, make that each city or village, has its own special recipe or a local riff on a regional dish. So there are plenty of options to choose from when cooking in your camper. Then again, we'd also advise you to eat out regularly – we did too. Some specialities are better eaten in a restaurant and usually dining out in Italy is surprisingly affordable.

BEANS THAT GO WITH EVERYTHING

The inland of Le Marche, which borders on Umbria, is the heartland of lentils and beans. You'll find beans on the menu in almost all restaurants. Served very simply, as a side, with a dash of stock or cooking liquid. We love beans so we always order a bowl with our tagliata.

Vegan
Serves 4

200 g dried cannellini beans
1 head of garlic
1 onion
3 bay leaves
10 black pepper corns
2 sprigs of thyme
splash of olive oil
1 tsp salt
1 lemon (zest, optional)

Soak the beans overnight in a large bowl with plenty of water. The next day, transfer the beans and the water to a pot. Add some more water.

Halve the head of garlic. No need to peel it. Peel and cut the onion in half. Add the garlic, the bay leaves, the peppercorns, the thyme, the onion, the olive oil and the salt to the pot and cook the beans for 30 minutes until done. The cooking time depends on the size of the beans so taste and check. The beans must be done, but not mushy.

Store the beans in the cooking liquid. Serve in some cooking liquid and season with black pepper. You can add some lemon zest if you want. Dip your bread in the liquid: it's absolutely delicious.

PA/TA E CECI

A good example of *cucina povera* and a typical farmer's dish from Le Marche. Pasta e ceci is neither a pasta, nor a soup and has many variations: sometimes it is made with stock and chickpeas, other times they blend the stock with half of the chickpeas for a more velvety sauce. That is what we will be doing in this recipe. We also serve it with *pangrattato* (grated bread), or the poor man's Parmesan as it's also known.

Serves 4

1 sweet onion
3 garlic cloves
1 sprig of rosemary
3 anchovy fillets
1 chilli
2 tbsp tomato purée
1 tin chickpeas (240 g drained)
1 l vegetable stock
200 g ditalini or other short pasta shapes
3 tbsp olive oil
pinch of salt

For the pangrattato
8 tbsp breadcrumbs
1 sprig of thyme
splash of olive oil
parsley (optional)

Peel and finely chop the onion and the garlic. Heat the oil in a casserole and fry the onion until translucent. Add the garlic, the rosemary, and the anchovy fillets and cook for 4 minutes. Finely slice the chilli and add it to the casserole. Add the tomato purée and cook while stirring for 3 minutes.

Drain the chickpeas and rinse thoroughly. Add half of the chickpeas to the casserole and cook. Pour in the stock and cook for 20 minutes. Boil the pasta in salted water.

Blend the chickpeas until smooth and add the remaining chickpeas. Season with salt and pepper. Drain the pasta and add it to the sauce.

Prepare the pangrattato. Fry the breadcrumbs until golden brown in a pan with olive oil. Add the thyme leaves and serve with the pasta. Garnish with some parsley if you want.

WILD BOAR RAGÙ

The nature in Le Marche is paradise for all kinds of game, which ultimately finds its way onto the plates of the locals. Wild boar is especially popular on restaurant menus. They often make ragù from it: a relatively dry, grainy meat sauce, and a traditional recipe (you can find our version on p. 120). Here the ragù has a unique, gamey taste, which will make any pasta dish even more delicious.

Serves 4

600 g boar fillet
500 ml red wine
2 bay leaves
2 sprigs of sage + 1 as garnish
10 black pepper corns
1 onion
2 carrots
2 celery stalks
2 garlic cloves
2 tbsp tomato purée
400 ml beef or wild game stock
400 g pasta of your choice
3 tbsp olive oil
salt and pepper

Add the bay leaves, 2 sprigs of sage and the peppercorns to the red wine. Marinate the boar fillet in the wine overnight.

Remove the meat from the marinade and cut into equal pieces. Strain the marinade and set aside.

Finely chop the onion and the garlic. Peel the carrots, wash the celery, and cut them into small pieces. Heat the oil in a large deep frying pan. Fry the onion until translucent. Add the garlic, the celery, and the carrots. Cook for at least 15 minutes.

Add the tomato purée to the vegetables and cook for 2 minutes. Add the meat and cook a little longer. Pour in the wine in which you marinated the meat and reduce for 5 minutes. Pour in the stock and cover with a lid. Simmer over low heat for 2 hours.

Check whether the meat is tender and whether you need to add more stock. Season with salt and pepper.

Cook the pasta until it's al dente in salted, boiling water. Drain and add to the ragù. Add a generous ladle of the cooking liquid, stir well, and garnish with shredded sage.

BLT WITH PORCHETTA

We love porchetta (and when we say love, we mean we are obsessed with the stuff).
We had our best porchetta ever in Le Marche: perfectly crispy on the outside,
melt in the mouth on the inside, with just the right seasoning. We found this heavenly porchetta
very randomly, on the road, in a tiny place, with long refrigerated counters, a few stools by
the bar, and a large roll of porchetta, covered with aluminium foil. Customers would roll up
with their oven dish to pick up some porchetta, much like we pick up a roast chicken
on Sundays in Belgium. If you're in Le Marche, do stop at a food truck or roadside tavern,
and walk in with an oven dish for some porchetta. Take it from us: it's simply irresistible.

In Le Marche, the Italians like to eat their porchetta in a sandwich roll with chilli –
because chilli is a regional product. A divine combination: so simple, yet so good!
This BLT with porchetta instead of bacon is the ideal camper lunch.

Serves 2

thick slices of bread of your choice
300 g porchetta
1 or 2 tomatoes
some cucumber slices
¼ head of Iceberg lettuce
2 tbsp mayonnaise
hot sauce to taste (optional)

Spread mayonnaise and hot sauce on the sliced bread,
add porchetta, tomato, cucumber and salad.

BRODETTO ALL'ANCONETANA

A brodetto is sort of like a fish soup, but looks more like a fish stew. There are various variants and recipes in Le Marche. This one, from Ancona, is especially tasty and has a special significance. The original recipe asks for 13 types of fish, symbolising Christ and his 12 apostles. If you want all of them, then order this soup in a restaurant. You'll agree with us that trying to prepare 13 different types of fish in a camper van is stretching it. We stick to the fish that is available for this recipe, pimping the original recipe, which is very pure and simple, to serve this flavour bomb.

Serves 4 to 6

1 onion
2 garlic cloves
3 anchovy fillets
3 l fish stock
1 tin chopped tomatoes
2 kg fish and shellfish of your choice,
    according to taste and/or availability
2 tbsp capers
30 baked black olives
2 lemons (zest and juice)
flat-leaf parsley
3 tbsp olive oil
salt and pepper
bread for dipping

Finely chop the onion and the garlic. Heat the oil in a casserole and fry the garlic and the onion until translucent. Add the anchovy fillets and stir until the fillets have dissolved.

Pour in the fish stock and add the chopped tomatoes. Simmer for 20 minutes over low heat. Season with salt and pepper.

Cut the fish into equal pieces and cook the fish and the shellfish in the brodetto according to size.

Finely slice one lemon, use the zest of the other. Add the sliced lemon, the olives, and the capers to the soup.

Cook for another 2 minutes. Finely chop the parsley. Garnish with lemon zest and parsley and season with salt and pepper. Serve with bread.

AFFOGATO

**The Italian iced coffee. You can't go wrong with this super simple dessert
in the country with the best coffee and the best gelato. Crumble in some biscotti
to add crunch and add a shot of amaretto for fans.**

Vegetarian
Serves 4

4 cups of your best coffee
4 scoops of vanilla ice cream
    from the local gelateria
almond biscotti
splash of amaretto (optional)

Scoop the ice cream into verrines or coffee cups. Pour over the coffee, and a shot of amaretto for anyone who wants. Crumble the biscotti over the ice cream and serve.

AMARENA CHERRY DESSERT

In a country where sweet treats abound, the Amarena cherry is the cherry on the cake. In Italy it is often served with gelato, but we prefer to pair these sour cherries in sugar syrup with mascarpone. We mix it with yoghurt and lemon juice for an airy, fresh dessert that will have you coming back for seconds.

Vegetarian
Serves 4

4 tbsp mascarpone
4 tbsp full fat yoghurt
½ lemon (juice)
4 tbsp Amarena cherries
4 tsp syrup of the glazed cherries
4 tbsp flaked almonds
4 ladyfinger or boudoir biscuits of your choice

Mix the mascarpone, the yoghurt, and the lemon juice in a bowl and scoop into the verrines. Add the cherries and the cherry syrup. Toast the flaked almonds in a pan until golden brown and serve with the cherries and the ladyfingers.

UMBRIA

Cascata delle Marmore

Umbria is situated next to stunning, famous and widely loved Tuscany but in recent years, it has emerged from its shadow as an equally popular destination for a dream holiday. It has fabulously beautiful villages and cities, excellent wines and superb regional products. Umbria (and neighbouring Le Marche) is famous for its truffles, pork and wild boar. The region's nature is also magnificent and very diverse: you'll run into rivers, waterfalls, lakes, beech forests, vineyards, olive groves, caves, hills, and mountains, which we think is a huge plus. The Apennines, the long spine that extends across Italy, run through Umbria. This is a top spot for walks, but perhaps not in summer. In times of heatwaves and draught, the region, which is known as the 'green heart of Italy', is extremely vulnerable to forest fires as we experienced first-hand… Thanks to the sirens of the fire trucks, we were able to find our way out of the forest very quickly, back to the inhabited world but we realise that things could have turned out very differently. So here's a tip: don't follow our example and never, and we really mean never, go for a walk in the forest when there's a risk of fire.

Monti Sibillini

If mountains are your thing: Monti Sibillini in the Apennines is one of the smaller national parks in Europe (just 70 hectares) but what a stunner it is. Download the AllTrails app and you're good to go for days of hiking with stunning views en route, such as the peaks of the Gran Sasso in the distance. We spent the night in a large campsite on the mountain, with three swimming pools and pitches with a view of the mountains.

One day of our holiday that was truly memorable was our visit to Assisi. While this is one of the tourist hotspots in Umbria, we can see why: the city with its old white-pinkish stone buildings sparkling on a hill in the landscape is simply magical. There are many traces of the legendary history of Assisi in the medieval centre, which only adds to the unique atmosphere. A sacred atmosphere even, because Assisi attracts tourists in search of beauty as well as many pilgrims who come here to pray to Saint Francis. Order a coffee in Piazza del Comune, admire the fountain with the three lions, and visit the Tempio di Minerva.

— Assisi

UMBRIA

Assisi

Monti Sibillini

Norcia

Terni

Some more nice spots

Fontemaggio is an excellent base for campers in Umbria, with lots of shady, quiet pitches for campers and a hotel, a hostel, two holiday cottages and a small supermarket. The campsite also accommodates the large buses in which pilgrims – often young people – travel to Assisi. One morning we woke up to them singing on the campsite: a priest was saying Mass for them. Definitely one of the more memorable mornings of our trip. Fontemaggio also has an amazing restaurant, where they cook on a wood fire. It is also very popular with people who are not staying at the campsite or in the hotel and who, like us, enjoy the chaos, filling their plates with delicious pasta and grilled meats. The ambience is cosy and welcoming, the wine good. We loved it here!
— Via Eremo delle Carceri 24, 06081 Assisi

A tiny trail leads from the campsite to Assisi, the birthplace of Saint Francis: the patron saint of Italy, the founder of the Franciscan order, and the patron saint of all animals and the environment. Do visit the **Basilica di San Francesco d'Assisi**: a unique three-part Gothic church, with the crypt with the tomb of Saint Francis, a simple lower church, and a brighter upper church. The ensemble is quite stunning, and the colours are especially beautiful and very different from other cathedrals and churches across Italy, which are usually resplendent with gold.
— Piazza Inferiore di San Francesco 2, 06081 Assisi

Assisi

Norcia, a walled city in east Umbria, at the foot of the Monti Sibillini, is known for its culinary delights. People flock here for the many *norcinerias*: traditional, usually tiny butcher's shops, with displays full of artisanal pork and boar delicacies. Park your car outside the city walls. In the city, you'll find beautiful historic streets and houses, many of which were unfortunately damaged during two earthquakes in 2016. They are being restored, with care and respect for their heritage value, which obviously takes time. Fortunately, the many amazing food shops and osterias are open. We tucked into charcuterie, cheese, lentils, spelt, and black truffles and concluded yet again that the fresh truffles from Umbria are truly delicious.

Another beautiful and popular attraction and a fun place to stop en route is the **Cascata delle Marmore**. This artificial waterfall (see the photo on p. 154) is an impressive 165 metres high and is just the place to cool down on a hot summer's day. There are various hiking trails that wind their way past the waterfall and a car park.

— 05100 Terni

FOOD

Umbria is famous for its pork and its wild boar. The pigs that are traditionally reared are fed acorns, maize, and grains, and you can taste the difference. The people here are tremendously proud of their *norcinerias*, the traditional butcher shops. The façades with their amazing window displays are really something else. Besides tasty meat, Umbria is also known for its lentils, beans and grains like farro. And... truffles, of course. Black summer truffle grows widely in Umbria, on the roots of hazelnut and oak trees. Here they call truffles 'black diamonds' or *il re della tavola* (the king of the dining table). Black truffles are not as elusive as white truffles, but they are still a rather costly delicacy. If you are travelling through Umbria, buying fresh truffles – or going truffle hunting with a guide – is a must. The excellent taste is nothing like the chemical and heavily scented truffle pastes that are used in so many industrial products.

TRUFFLE AND EGGS

**We would happily eat these eggs for breakfast every morning!
At the risk of sounding repetitive, you really should buy truffles when you're on holiday
in Umbria. They are less expensive than you think and even tastier than you thought.
Don't keep them in a sealed storage container as they tend to grow mouldy.**

Vegetarian
Serves 4

4 to 6 eggs
1 tbsp dairy butter
fresh seasonal truffle
salt and pepper

Crack the eggs and beat them. Heat the butter in a frying pan and season with salt and pepper. Pour the egg mixture into the frying pan and use a fork to slowly push the edges of the eggs to the centre. Don't stir or scramble them.

Once most of the raw egg has set, remove the folded eggs from the pain. They will continue to cook so don't let them sit in the warm pan. Garnish with as much shaved truffle as you want and serve with a slice of bread.

LENTIL STEW WITH GUANCIALE AND PECORINO

Umbria's local speciality with some of the best ingredients that this region has to offer: lentils, pecorino and, especially, guanciale. The latter is matured and salted pork, cut from the cheek or jowl – from *guancia*, the Italian word for cheek.

Serves 4

100 g guanciale
1 onion
1 garlic clove
1 celery stalk
2 carrots
400 g lentils
1 sprig of rosemary
2 bay leaves
150 ml white wine
1½ l beef stock
80 g pecorino
4 tbsp olive oil
salt and pepper

Cut the guanciale into small cubes. Finely chop the onion and the garlic. Wash the celery and cut it into small pieces. Peel and dice the carrots.

Heat the oil in a casserole and fry the guanciale until it is just turning brown. Add the onion, the celery, and the carrots. Cook for 15 minutes.

Add the garlic and stir well. Cook for 2 minutes. Then add the lentils, the rosemary, the bay leaves, and the white wine. Pour over the stock and cook until the lentils are tender. Season with salt and pepper. Add some grated pecorino before serving.

LINGUINE WITH FENNEL SAUSAGES AND MUSHROOMS

We ate this pasta dish several times during our holiday in Italy. It's simple and surprisingly tasty. Great for a camping holiday. In this instance, we used fennel sausages, but you can basically use any minced meat.

Serves 4

60 g pancetta or guanciale
2 onions
2 garlic cloves
1 celery stalk
250 g mushrooms
1 kg fennel sausages
100 ml white wine
400 g linguine
2 tbsp olive oil
salt and pepper

Cut the pancetta or the guanciale into small cubes. Finely chop the onion and the garlic. Wash the celery and cut it into small pieces. Clean the mushrooms and quarter them.

Heat the oil in a frying pan and fry the guanciale or pancetta until it is just turning brown. Fry the mushrooms. Add the garlic, the onions, and the celery and cook for 15 minutes.

Remove the sausage casings and cook the meat until it is done and crispy. Add the white wine and allow the alcohol to evaporate.

In the meantime, cook the pasta until al dente. Add the pasta to the minced meat. Add some pasta water and stir well. Season with salt and pepper and serve!

CACIO E PEPE

Less is more and this fine example of *cucina povera* is the living proof of this. Originally this is a recipe from Lazio, the region around Rome; we've included it here in the Umbria chapter because we feel our book wouldn't be complete without it, and the ingredients are available everywhere in Italy. All you need for this dish is pepper and cheese, and a good amount of culinary passion and dedication.

Vegetarian
Serves 2

100 g spaghetti
6 g black peppercorns
50 g pecorino
20 g Parmesan cheese

Crush the peppercorns with a mortar and pestle. Toast them in a dry pan to release the fragrance and flavour.

Boil the pasta for 3 minutes in salted water. Add 2 ladles of the pasta water to the pepper in the pan and reduce.

Add the pasta and another 2 ladles of pasta water. Stir and toss well so the sauce coats the pasta until the pasta is al dente.

Grate the cheese and gradually sprinkle it over the pasta, alternating with the pasta water, to obtain a creamy sauce. Serve immediately.

HUGO SPRITZ & ROSSINI

What would Italy be without prosecco! These two easy cocktails take just minutes to make.

For 1 hugo spritz

80 ml prosecco
80 ml sparkling water
40 ml elderflower syrup
some mint leaves
slice of lemon

Combine the prosecco, the sparkling water, and the syrup in a large glass and add some ice cubes. Garnish with the lemon slice and the mint leaves.

For 1 rossini

100 ml prosecco
2 strawberries
1 tsp sugar
3 basil leaves

Muddle the strawberries and sugar. Transfer the strawberry purée to a glass and pour over the prosecco. Add some ice cubes and garnish with the basil leaves.

PIT STOP: LAZIO

Lazio is home to Rome, the capital of Italy, and the reason why so many foreign tourists head to the region as part of a city trip to the Eternal City. While we can see why, we also think it's a bit sad because Lazio has so much more to offer: Lake Bolsena or Lake Vico, the Etruscan necropolis in the papal city of Viterbo, the gardens of Villa Lante in Bagnaia and Villa d'Este in Tivoli are all worth visiting. More to the south, you can unwind on the pristine beaches between picturesque San Felice Circeo and Sperlonga. The twelve villages of the Castelli Romani (the 'Roman castles') in the Alban hills are a must-see.

We made a pit stop at **International Glamping Lago di Bracciano**, which is just 30 minutes from Rome by car. This stunning lake is actually a gigantic volcanic crater, which was filled with water 600,000 years ago after several eruptions. The campsite has a private beach on the lake – with black volcanic sand! – and a small swimming pool (swimming cap mandatory), lots of playground equipment for kids, a good restaurant and bar and clean sanitary facilities. There's a nice shop on the opposite side of the street where you can pick up fresh fruit and veg. A great place to relax, swim, and cook among a largely Italian crowd.

— Via del Pianoro 4, 00069 Trevignano Romano

Glamping Lago di Bracciano

Lake Bracciano

ABRUZZO

National Park Gran Sasso e Monti della Laga

National Park Gran Sasso e Monti della Laga

The mountainous region of Abruzzo forms a transition zone between central and southern Italy and is an upcoming holiday destination. It's easy to see why when you look at the amazing scenic landscapes. Extra special: you can smell the sea in the mountains and see the peaks from the beach as you look inland. Here getting from the sea to the rocky hilltops takes just an hour by car. The rugged terrain of the Apennines is lined with mountain lakes and rivers, and is home to many wild creatures, including eagles, wild goats, wolves and even brown bears. If you decide to spend the night in your camper van, remember not to leave your garbage out at night, and it may be worth your while to close your doors and windows. We realise that we're beginning to sound like a broken record, but holy moly, when you drive land inwards from the beach, up and down the mountains, you can't help but marvel in silence at the landscape around you. It also seems like a great region for a motorcycle tour. We were blown away by Gran Sasso National Park – Gran Sasso means Great Rock. This vast massif has been likened to Tibet and to be fair, you wouldn't expect to come across this kind of pristine, rugged scenery in Italy but there you have it. The same applies to the 'white wolves' that randomly cross your path. Fortunately, these big white dogs – because that's what they are – help shepherds herd the flocks to their summer pastures as the seasons change.

Gran Sasso e Monti della Laga National Park is so vast that you won't run into too many people there, besides the odd passionate hiker. It feels both desolate and exciting. So you can imagine how surprised we were when we came upon a market stall in the middle of nowhere, with some lovely veg displayed on tiny tables. Up the road, we spot another farmer with an impressive moustache and an equally impressive gold chain, who is selling his home-made pecorino. One of the most popular cheeses in Italy, this sheep cheese is made all over Abruzzo. The cheese is aged for anything from a couple of weeks to a year, bringing out different flavours. The strongest pecorino that we bought from a roadside stall in Abruzzo was simply mind-blowing: we haven't tasted anything like it since then.

— Gran Sasso d'Italia

On the way to Castel del Monte

On the way to our campsite, we spotted a scene that made us look twice: out of nowhere, on the mountain plateau, a group of people – on bicycles, motorcycles, in camper vans ... – had assembled. It's only when we got closer that we realised what was going on: a barbecue. Much to our joy, we found a butcher's shop/improvised restaurant in the mountains, with thirty or so barbecues for arrosticini or grilled lamb or mutton skewers (see also p. 195), a traditional regional dish. Over the years, customers used to run into each other in the butcher's shop and hang around for a chat. One day, they decided to throw some meat on the barbecue and that is how an excellent custom was born. All you need to do is choose your meat, the butcher wraps it in paper, and throws in some bread and a tomato. Then you order a drink, pick a barbecue, and grill your meat while you chat with the person at the grill next to you. An unbeatable holiday experience!

Parco nazionale del
Gran Sasso e Monti della Laga

●— Gran Sasso d'Italia

Castel del Monte —●

●— Santo Stefano di Sessanio
●— Calascio

●— Sant'Eufemia a Maiella

ABRUZZO

Parco nazionale
della Maiella

Some more nice spots

In Gran Sasso National Park (or Parco nazionale del Gran Sasso e Monti della Laga, its official name), we settled on Campo Imperatore near the pretty town of **Castel del Monte** to park our camper van for the night. Apparently, the region used to be very popular with directors of spaghetti westerns once upon a time. Our campsite became the set for a Bud Spencer flick.
—— Via di Campo Imperatore, 67023 Castel del Monte

The famous **Rocca Calascio** is one of Italy's oldest preserved fortresses. Its location, on one of Abruzzo's highest mountain peaks, amid a rugged landscape, is simply breathtaking. The rock and the castle have previously been used as film sets. *Ladyhawke* and *The Name of the Rose* were filmed here.
—— 67020 Calascio

—— Castel del Monte

Santo Stefano di Sessanio

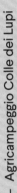
Agricampeggio Colle dei Lupi

If you visit one thing in Abruzzo, then our top recommendation would be the medieval town of **Santo Stefano di Sessanio**. Like so many other towns in this region, it was severely damaged in the 2009 earthquake in L'Aquila. Afterwards, the population left in droves. The town is currently being rebuilt with the greatest respect for heritage but it is a very slow-moving process. In recent years, the town has become more lively after a property developer launched a unique renovation project: he bought almost all of the houses in the village, and combined them into one hotel with several rooms and spaces in different streets. It may not sound like it, but it is incredibly beautiful, and you don't even notice that it's a hotel, except for one tiny reception area which is tucked away in a narrow alley.

Agricampeggio Colle dei Lupi is located at the foot of Montagne del Morrone in Maiella National Park. This is the kind of campsite we dream of opening ourselves. Simply heavenly. We can't think of any downsides: the sanitation facilities are simple and good, the pitches (there are 40 in all) are perfect and are all situated in the shade, and the swimming pool is amazing. What we appreciated most of all, however, was the passion with which it was run. Felice, the friendly host, explained that he built the campsite for Alicia, the love of his life and his wife, who followed her heart fifty years ago and moved from the USA to Italy. We would have loved to spend more time with Felice and Alicia: we really enjoyed the wonderful hikes in the region, the calm, and the tasty food – Felice rang the nearby restaurant, which opened its doors especially for us – and the wonderful ambience in the village, where the nonnas chat in the grocery shop.
— Contrada San Giacomo, 65020 Sant'Eufemia a Maiella Pescara

FOOD

Abruzzo's regional cuisine is all about bold flavours. Many of the region's culinary traditions originated in the mountains where the sheep graze. Lamb is a recurring ingredient as is Pecorino, the hard cheese made from sheep's milk and a local speciality. Abruzzo is also known for its wheat. They produce various rustic breads and, of course, lots of pasta here. According to the Abruzzesi, the superior quality of their wheat, combined with the purest water, produces the best dried pasta. Global pasta brand De Cecco produces its range at the foot of the majestic Maiella mountains. We have included two seafood recipes in this chapter as well, because Abruzzo borders on the Adriatic.

INSALATA DI POLPO

Squid, truly one of our most-loved ingredients ... This polpo salad, and its many variations, is the salad of dreams and one of our favourite Mediterranean dishes. This simple dish takes just minutes to prepare and instantly conjures up that holiday feeling: another tasty recipe to add to your camping recipe book. Don't forget to pop a bottle of prosecco in the fridge.

Serves 2 as a main course
or 4 as a starter

200 g precooked octopus tentacles
1 red onion
approx. 15 cherry tomatoes
approx. 10 black olives
½ bunch of flat-leaf parsley
1 tbsp capers
1 garlic clove
1 lemon (juice)
pinch of cayenne pepper
3 tbsp olive oil
salt and pepper

Cut the tentacles into bitesize pieces. Peel and cut the onion into half-moons. Halve the cherry tomatoes and the black olives. Finely chop the parsley.

Combine all these ingredients, add the capers, and grate and add the garlic. Drizzle with olive oil and lemon juice. Season with salt, pepper, and cayenne pepper.

COZZE GRATINATE

Gratinated mussels always make for a nice snack or appetizer, but they are difficult to prepare in a camper van. We came up with this camper-friendly version, using our favourite Italian solution, pangrattato. We use these crispy, flavoured breadcrumbs in several recipes in this book that could do with a bit of crunch. Here it is a perfect alternative to a gratin.

Serves 4

500 g fresh mussels
1 onion
2 garlic cloves
1 tbsp tomato purée
1 glass white wine
salt and pepper

For the pangrattato
6 tbsp breadcrumbs
½ bunch of flat-leaf parsley
1 tbsp olive oil

Rinse the mussels with cold water. Finely chop the onion and the garlic. Heat the oil in a casserole and fry the garlic and the onion until translucent. Add the tomato purée and cook for 2 minutes over low heat. Pour the white wine into the casserole and let the alcohol evaporate.

Toss in the mussels and cook them for 5 minutes or until they open. Shake the mussels well and season with salt and pepper.

Fry the breadcrumbs in the olive oil and finely chop the parsley. Combine the parsley with the breadcrumbs. Transfer the mussels to a serving dish and scoop a teaspoon of pangrattato on each of the mussels.

ARROSTICINI

A superb example of great street food: these lamb or mutton skewers are a traditional delicacy from Abruzzo. You can find these all over Central Italy at the local *macelleria* (butcher) where they grill these skewers on the spot for you, serving them with a side of bread and tomatoes.

Serves 4

300 g of lamb meat or mutton
    (may be quite fatty, for more flavour)
4 skewers or branches of rosemary
2 ripe tomatoes
bread to taste
hot sauce
salt and pepper

Cut the meat into smaller pieces and stick them on a skewer or a branch of rosemary. Season with salt and pepper.

Grill the meat skewers over a wood fire. Serve with bread, tomatoes, and a hot sauce of your choice.

LAMB STEW WITH OLIVES AND PANGRATTATO

This stew (which we serve with, yes you've guessed it, pangrattato) is a real flavour bomb. We call it the one pot wonder. Lamb, lemon, olives, sage, and red wine: potent flavours that are a match made in heaven. A bowl of this stew, on your lap, on a cooler evening under a blanket near the campfire, with the sun setting behind the mountains: sounds like the perfect holiday dinner to us.

Serves 4

600 g lamb meat
    (lamb neck, breast, deboned shoulder...
    as long as it's fatty)
2 onions
4 garlic cloves
1 red chilli
1 lemon (the peel)
2 sprigs of sage
2 bay leaves
1 tin of peeled tomatoes
200 ml red wine
200 ml lamb stock (or beef stock)
400 g waxy potatoes
100 g black olives
3 tbsp olive oil

For the pangrattato
4 tbsp breadcrumbs
3 sage leaves
1 tbsp olive oil

Cut the lamb into bite-sized pieces. Finely chop the onion and the garlic. Finely slice the chilli. Peel the lemon and reserve the peel (without the pith).

Heat the oil in a large, deep frying pan. Sear the meat on all sides and remove it from the pan. Fry the garlic, the onion, and the chilli in the meat fat.

Return the meat to the pan, and add the sage, the bay leaves, and the lemon peel. Cook for 5 minutes. Pour the red wine into the pan and let the alcohol evaporate. Add the peeled tomatoes, crush with a spoon, then pour over the stock. Cover and simmer for an hour or so over low heat. Stir now and then and add more water if needed.

Peel the potatoes and quarter them. Add the potatoes to the meat after 1 hour and cook them in the stew. Halve the olives and add them to the stew.

Make the pangrattato: heat the oil in a frying pan and fry the breadcrumbs until golden brown. Mince the sage leaves and add them to the breadcrumbs.

Check whether the meat is succulent and tender, and the potatoes are done. Serve the stew with the pangrattato.

SCRIPPELLE 'MBUSSE

**We know what we will be dishing up for our grandchildren on Wednesday afternoons...
These savoury pancakes are ridiculously tasty. They're somewhat similar
to the German or Austrian fritattensuppe, but much better.**

Vegetarian
Serves 4

50 g flour
6 eggs
1 l whole milk
150 g pecorino
1½ l hot chicken stock
butter for frying
salt and pepper

Place the flour in a large mixing bowl and add the eggs. Stir while you gently pour in the milk. Season with salt and pepper and let the batter rest for 20 minutes.

Heat the butter in a frying pan and cook the pancakes. While cooking, sprinkle some grated pecorino on the pancakes and roll them up.

Place 2 to 3 pancakes per person in a deep dish and pour over the hot chicken stock.

PASTA ALLA CHITARRA

Spaghetti alla chitarra literally means 'guitar spaghetti'. The name has nothing to do with the musical instrument, instead it refers to the tool that you use to make this pasta. Like a guitar, it has a frame with a series of parallel wires crossing, through which you press the dough. This simple dish is a regional speciality of Abruzzo and is prepared with just a few ingredients. This also means that your choice of products can make or break your dish: so buy the ripest, sweetest tomatoes and the best burrata you can get your hands on.

Vegetarian
Serves 2

1 onion
1 garlic clove
1 red chilli
300 g cherry tomatoes
250 g pasta alla chitarra
1 bunch of basil
1 burrata ball
60 g hazelnuts, chopped
4 tbsp olive oil

Finely chop the onion and the garlic. Heat the oil in a pan and fry the garlic and the onion until translucent. Finely slice the chilli and add it to the onion mixture. Next, add the tomatoes, cover, and simmer for 10 minutes.

Cook the pasta until it's al dente in salted, boiling water. Drain and add to the sauce. Add two ladles of the pasta water.

Shred the basil leaves into the pasta and toss well. Season with salt and pepper. Transfer the pasta to a plate and place a ball of burrata on top of it. Serve with chopped hazelnuts.

AUBERGINE DIP

This recipe is all about time. It is crucial that you give the mixture plenty of time to simmer so the flavours can develop. Fortunately, time is never an issue when you're on holiday, right? This dip also pairs nicely as a sauce with pasta, meat, or grilled veg.

Serves 4

1 aubergine
1 sweet onion
1 garlic clove
1 red chilli
2 anchovy fillets
400 g peeled tomatoes
½ lemon (zest)
1 sprig of flat-leaf parsley
3 tbsp olive oil
bread for dipping

Cut the onion into half-moons and press the garlic. Finely slice the chilli. Wash the aubergine and chop into small cubes. Heat the oil in a pan and fry the aubergines for 10 minutes until golden brown.

Add the onion, the pressed garlic, the anchovy fillets, and the chilli. Cook for another 10 minutes until the onion has softened. Add the tomatoes to the pan and crush them with your spoon. Cover and simmer for 40 minutes. Give it a good stir now and then.

Transfer the dip to a plate and garnish with some lemon zest and coarsely chopped parsley. Serve with bread.

COFFEE ZABAGLIONE

**There are no words to describe this Italian coffee-based dessert.
Perhaps simply divine will do?**

Vegetarian
Serves 4

5 egg yolks
2 capfuls of granulated sugar
3 capfuls of amaretto
strong coffee

Place the egg yolks in a saucepan and use the eggshell as your cap measure. Add the sugar and the amaretto to the egg yolks and beat.

Cook over very low heat and whisk constantly while the mixture becomes foamy. Turn your saucepan around now and then, to make sure you get the mixture on all the sides and don't end up with an omelette.

Prepare a cup of coffee for everyone and scoop the sabayon onto the coffee.

CAMPANIA

Sorrento

Campania is a great region for holidaymakers, if you don't mind searing hot temperatures that is. The capital is Naples; in recent years, this port has become an increasingly popular holiday destination and not just because there is a wide selection of (cheapish) flights to choose from. From Naples, you can visit Pompei, the ancient Roman city at the foot of Vesuvius, which was destroyed when the volcano erupted. But ask ten people which part of Campania you should really visit, and we think at least eight of them will answer 'the Amalfi coast', and they are right! Centuries-old towns line the steep cliffs along this rugged, rocky coastline – some of them are positioned almost perpendicular to the rocks – with spectacular views of the Tyrrhenian Sea. Breathtakingly beautiful and almost impossible to reach with most means of transport. Don't even bother trying with anything bigger than a Vespa or Fiat 500, because the narrow, winding coastal road is almost impossible to navigate. In our opinion, if you leave Naples with your camper van and head south towards the Penisola Sorrentina (the Sorrento Peninsula), Sorrento is as far as you'll get without accidents. Fortunately, this bustling seaside resort with its picturesque streets lined with shops and restaurants more than makes up for this. It's also a great place to charter a boat for an unforgettable boat trip to Amalfi and other seaside gems.

The Amalfi coast is both spectacular and heavenly, with its crystal-clear blue water, imposing rocky outcrops, and pastel towns that are built vertically against the cliffs. The coastline was listed as Unesco World Heritage in 1996 because of its natural beauty and cultural-historical value. The entire strip between Sorrento and Salerno is known as the Amalfi coast, but in effect, the actual coast is limited to thirteen towns between Positano and Vietri sul Mare.

You would do well to visit them by boat, largely because you avoid having to take a long bus ride on a very narrow, winding road. The drivers have to perform all kinds of crazy manoeuvres, which, in our case, caused our kids to be car sick. Secondly, because the best angle to see these towns is from the sea. You also sail past what is possibly the most picturesque site on the Amalfi coast. Fiordo del Furore is a tiny beach in a bay, and definitely worth a stop because of the unique view of the bridge over water on the coastal road.

Sorrento

Marina Grande in Sorrento

Sorrento is a friendly, touristy town, ideally suited to families: lots of good pizzas and ice creams for children and shellfish and seafood (in pasta, salads, or deep-fried) and limoncello spritz for parents. It even has a beach, which may sound less obvious than you think. Even though the sea is everywhere you look, Campania's rocky beaches are less suited if you were hoping to enjoy a beach holiday. In Sorrento, you can use the stairs or a lift to make your way down the steep, 50-metre-tall rocky outcrop and reach the tiny beaches. Most of them are private, however. You need to pay and you need to book your sun lounger well in advance! Marina Grande, a tiny bay near the centre of Sorrento, is the exception to the rule: this public beach is a great place for a refreshing dip in the sea and to relax or play in the sand among the locals.

Positano

The coastline is named after the largest town, Amalfi, which is also its historic and cultural centre. An 11th-century church, in the Sicilian-Arab style, dominates the picturesque streets and squares. But the other villages and towns are also worth visiting. Take Positano, where the basilica's cupola, which is clad with ceramics, sparkles in the sunlight and where lovely gardens and terraces have been built among the houses. Each town has its own ambience and character but they are all the same in that they offer lots of lovely terraces, delicious gelato, great wine, and plenty of shops where you can shop for ceramic tiles, limoncello or other local products. Preferably made of or decorated with lemons, the regional speciality. Here there are lemons everywhere you look: on the trees, on your plate, and on souvenirs. Don't even consider leaving Amalfi without having sampled one of our favourite desserts: a lemon filled with lemon sorbet!

Capri

The lovely island of Capri is situated just 30 minutes from Sorrento by boat. You can buy a ticket for a return trip but you can also take a trip around the island, which is really worth it. The boat will take you past Sophia Loren's house and the old lighthouse, through the natural arches of the Faraglioni, and tide permitting into the famous blue, white, and green grotto. The cherry on the cake is a dive off the boat and into the sea, just before you re-enter the harbour of Capri. In Anacapri, you can take the chair lift to the island's highest point with memorable panoramic views. It's easy to see why so many stars and jetsetters have a luxurious pad on this island …

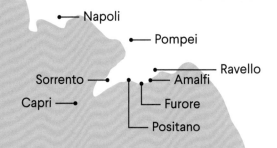

CAMPANIA

Napoli

Pompei

Ravello

Sorrento

Amalfi

Capri

Furore

Positano

Some more nice spots

Nube d'Argento is a lovely, terraced campsite in Sorrento, within walking distance of the beach and the town centre. Although relatively large, the many different tiers of this site and the olive trees make it feel more like a cosy, family campsite. The pitches under and among the trees are deliciously shady, with expansive views thrown in for free. Ours looked out onto the Bay of Naples, with Mount Vesuvius in the distance. Additional bonuses? The tiny but great pool, the campsite's restaurant with a wood-fired pizza oven and the information booth at reception where you can book all kinds of excursions.

— Via Capo 21, 80067 Sorrento

— Nube d'Argento

Pompei

Ravello is definitely in the running for the most scenic town of the Amalfi coast. And these two amazing historic villas are partly to blame for this. Today **Villa Cimbrone** is an exclusive high-end hotel, but the beautifully designed English gardens are open to visitors. Gaze at the expansive views of the cliffs and boats from the enchanting Terrazzo dell'Infinito. The gardens of **Villa Rufolo**, where the famous composer Richard Wagner once stayed, are even more magical. Every year, they organise a music festival here.

•—— Via Santa Chiara 26 & Piazza Duomo 1, 84010 Ravello

At **Da Adolfo** your negroni is served right up to your lounger, in the shade of a matching parasol. On the menu: grilled mozzarella on lemon leaves, home-made tiramisu and much more goodies. The tiny bay is easiest to reach by boat; if you choose to come over land, brace yourself for a challenging descent through the shrubbery.

•—— Via Laurito 40, 84017 Positano

The Roman ruins of **Pompei** at the foot of Mount Vesuvius were covered under a thick layer of lava in 79 AD during an eruption. Today the site is home to some of the best preserved remnants of Roman antiquity. Definitely on the list of places to stop if you want to see what you learned in history lessons in real-life. A great way to visit Pompei is to book a coach trip from the campsite. All kinds of options are possible: a full day trip including a visit to the museum, a half day without a guide, with or without a meal … We had lunch in the restaurant of a winery on the flanks of Vesuvius. We also stopped at the Limoncello restaurant for a tasting on our way back: we had an amazing day!

Chez Black is an institution where fresh seafood is served by merry men in a sailor shirt. A favourite among many Italian and non-Italian VIPs.

•—— Via del Brigantino 19, 84017 Positano

•—— Garden of a Ravello villa

FOOD

In our humble opinion, the delicious cuisine of the Amalfi Coast can be summarised with two words: lemons and seafood. The latter makes sense, as the region is known for its coastline, and fresh fish is caught daily to supply the restaurants on the rocks. But the real wealth of this region are its lemons, which have been harvested for over 2000 years from trees which look like they're on the verge of collapsing under the weight of all the fruit. The local variety, the *sfusato amalfitano*, is slightly sweeter than the lemons you find in Belgium and the Netherlands. They are also very fragrant, have a thick, edible peel, and produce lots of juice that tastes less bitter and even sweeter. Perfect for lemonade, limoncello, and cooking!

PASTA AL LIMONE

Another divine example of Italian cuisine starring the yellow gold of Campania, aka lemons! The list of ingredients is short, but the method is less straightforward than you may think. Do not – we repeat, do not! – even think of adding cream: over our dead bodies!

Serves 4

2 garlic cloves
1 chilli
4 anchovy fillets
4 lemons (zest and juice)
1 bunch of basil
80 g Parmesan cheese
500 g spaghetti
4 tbsp olive oil
pepper

Coarsely chop the basil and finely slice the garlic and the chilli. Heat the oil in a large frying pan and fry the garlic with the chilli. Add the anchovies and stir until dissolved.

Squeeze the lemons and pour half of the lemon juice into the pan. Stir well. In the meantime, cook your pasta. Set the timer for 2 minutes less than the package instructions recommend.

Add the pasta to the lemon mixture and stir well. Then add 3 ladles of the pasta water and give the pasta a good stir so it absorbs the liquid. Now add the remaining lemon juice, the basil, and the grated Parmesan cheese.

Season with pepper. Sprinkle some lemon zest over the pasta, and serve!

PASTA ALLE VONGOLE

Pasta alle vongole has to be our favourite dish in the world and we think most people are inclined to agree with us. This is the classic way of preparing it. We don't add tomato or any other ingredients which – in our humble opinion – don't really belong in this dish anyway. Instead of clams (vongole), you can use the shellfish or seafood that you like best or that is available in shops or at the market.

Serves 4

1 onion
2 garlic cloves
2 chillis
1 kg vongole (small clams)
½ bunch of flat-leaf parsley
400 g linguini or spaghetti
100 ml olive oil
salt

Finely chop the onion and the garlic. Finely slice the chillis. Rinse the clams twice. Finely chop the parsley. In the meantime, cook your pasta. Set the timer for 2 minutes less than the package instructions recommend.

Heat the oil in a large frying pan and fry the garlic and the onion with the chillis. Tip the clams into the pan and give everything a good shake. Put the lid on the pan. Don't let them cook for too long.

Add the pasta to the clams and stir or toss well. Sprinkle with some parsley leaves and season with salt. Toss again and serve.

CEVICHE ALL'AMALFITANA

This squid ceviche with lots of lemon (you can never have too much lemon!) is a homage to the Amalfi coast and another example of the never-ending, delicious culinary uses of the fresh products that you can snap up in the coastal towns of Southern Italy, which are always of the highest quality.

Serves 4

250 g squid
(tubes or tentacles, preferably seppia)
½ fennel
2 lemons
chilli powder
½ bunch of basil
4 tbsp olive oil (extra virgin)
salt and pepper

Cut the squid into thin strips. Shave the fennel and slice the lemon on a mandoline.

Arrange the fennel and the lemon on a platter, then place the squid strips on top. Drizzle with olive oil and the juice of the other lemon. Season with salt, pepper, and chilli powder.

Refrigerate for 20 minutes. Garnish with basil just before serving.

NEGRONI

We dedicate this recipe to our amazing, funny, sweet, and intelligent friend and neighbour, the artist Bruno Roels. This is his favourite cocktail and obviously he has excellent taste.

For 1 negroni

30 ml Campari
30 ml Martini rosso
30 ml gin
slice of mandarin or orange
ice cubes

Pour all the ingredients into a glass. Add the ice cubes and garnish with a slice of mandarin or orange. Squeeze some lemon peel above the glass to express the citrus oil for a nice finishing touch.

CAPRI SPRITZ

This seductive summer drink looks like lemonade and tastes like a great thirst-quencher ... But it's the adult equivalent of lemonade. It tastes even better with an Italian playlist on in the background.

For 1 Capri spritz

75 ml prosecco
50 ml limoncello
25 ml sparkling water
crushed ice
1 lemon (peel)
1 sprig of mint

Pour the prosecco, the limoncello, and the sparkling water into a large glass. Add the crushed ice and garnish with the lemon peel and a sprig of mint.

PS
Squeeze the lemon peel to release a burst of citrus essence. Place the mint leaves or sprig in one hand gently smack it with your other to extract the oils.

LAST BUT NOT LEAST: PUGLIA

Puglia is situated in Italy's 'heel', in the south of the country. Meaning it can also get hot in summer – and we mean really hot, with temperatures easily reaching 40+ degrees. We hesitated about driving this far with our camper van, but we are very happy that we decided to push ahead in the end and experience its authentic ambience, with white villages instead of the pink terracotta houses of the north, and olive trees as far as the eye can see.

We spent the night at **Bosco Selva** – a tiny campsite with many trees and lots of shade – near **Alberobello**, a city with over 1,000 *trulli*. These small white limestone structures with their odd conical roofs are synonymous with Puglia. They are decorated with all kinds of religious and/ or mysterious pagan-like symbols to ward off evil. Alberobello can be quite busy and touristy. Steer clear of the Rione Monti area and walk towards Rione Aia Picolla instead. This neighbourhood is much less commercialised, and it also has many charming trulli.

— Via Bosco Selva 25, 70011 Alberobello

— Alberobello

To be fair, all of Puglia's white towns are worthy of your time. We took a stroll through the narrow streets of **Locorotondo** and **Martina Franca**, where we enjoyed the serene atmosphere that emanated from the whitewashed houses, beating the heat by visiting the local churches and admiring their interiors, with all the gold and the frescoes. If, like us, you tend to follow your nose when travelling, stop in charming **Cisternino** where you'll find that many butchers have an adjoining dining area with grills, like in Abruzzo. Do taste the famous *bombette*, a local speciality of rolled pork stuffed with melted cheese and pancetta. The perfect street food, on a rosemary skewer, with some bread on the side.

Last but not least: **Lecce**. The capital of Baroque architecture is like a big outdoor museum with a high cool factor. What's more, the sea is nearby, which is always good for a refreshing dip. We went surfing during the day, heading into the city at dusk, where we happened to gatecrash a religious procession and watched the sun set from the gigantic Piazza del Duomo. Another memorable holiday experience!

Lecce

Locorotondo

THANKS

To my favourite co-traveller and my everything: for going on road trips together, exploring, eating, hiking, doing nothing with the same passion and curiosity all these years. We do it better than anyone else together.

To Willy. If you read this, sorry mon amourke pour toujourke for the heat.

To Loulou and Dries: for letting us go on a trip for so long and taking such good care of grandma in the meantime. You rule! Although not having you around wasn't always easy: will you join us again soon, pretty please?

To Mum: for being there for us and ensuring that we could enjoy this trip without a care in the world.

To Jonathan and Jocelyne: for all the tips!

To Bramski and Stefania, our mates. We are so happy that we get to do so many fun projects together. Because we can!

To team Luster: nothing but love for you!

And to you, Dad: I would have loved to have been able to share all this with you. I miss you.

2022 was a tough, but tremendously beautiful year. A year of focussing on the essence of things. Here's to life!

Els

Firstly, to my partner and best friend Stephanie: our journey was a great story, although finding some peace and quiet with three small kids in our wake wasn't always as easy as we would have liked it to be. Love you 4Ever, Gigi Boubou 4Life.

To my three lovely children, Lena, Liv and Loulou, for always being up for a new adventure.

To my parents, for all the support, and to my sister and her family. To Auntie Bei and Jan for all the catsitting. Family first!

To Els and her family, for being so much more than a co-worker. I already look forward to our next project as a dream team.

To Jelle, for exploring Amalfi with me. Pistachio ice cream, pasta, and inspiration for life…
To Andy and his superb camper van: if you ever consider selling it, call me baby!

To Vanomobil Deerlijk, for supplying my new, future campervan in mint condition and (spoiler alert!) for renting us the camper van for our next Camperfood Winter book!

And finally, to the entire team at Luster: thanks for the great collaboration.

Bram

CAMPER FOOD & STORIES
ITALY

Recipes
Els Sirejacob

Composition and texts
Els Sirejacob and Bram Debaenst

Photography
Bram Debaenst and Els Sirejacob

Graphic design
Sarah Schrauwen (doublebill.design)

Editing
Hadewijch Ceulemans

Translation
Sandy Logan

(Original title: *Camperfood & fijne plekken – Italië*)

D/2023/12.005/9
ISBN 9789460583414
NUR 500, 440

© 2023 Luster, Antwerp
lusterpublishing.com

All rights reserved.
No part of this publication may be reproduced, stored in a retrieval system,
or transmitted, in any form or by any means, without the prior written consent
of the publisher. An exception is made for short excerpts which may be cited
for the sole purpose of reviews.